ROUGH
GUIDES

T0085812

POCKET **ROUGH GUIDE**
STOCKHOLM

written and researched by
ANNIE WARREN

CONTENTS

STOCKHOLM

Without a shadow of a doubt, Stockholm is one of Europe's most beautiful cities. Built on no fewer than fourteen islands connected by fifty-seven bridges, where the fresh water of Lake Mälaren meets the brackish Baltic Sea, clean air and open space are in plentiful supply here. One-third of the area within the city limits is made up of water, while another third comprises parks and woodlands. As a result, the capital is one of Europe's saner cities and a delightful place in which to spend time. Broad boulevards lined with elegant buildings are reflected in the deep blue water, and rows of painted wooden houseboats bob gently alongside the cobbled waterfront. Yet Stockholm is also a high-tech metropolis, with futuristic skyscrapers, a bustling commercial heart and one of the world's hottest start-up scenes.

Looking out over Strömmen from the restaurant at Fotografiska

When to visit

Stockholm is a year-round destination, blessed with all four seasons to their fullest extent. The spring season of March to May is often the driest, and bars will start to use their outside terraces – though you'll still need a coat to use them comfortably and the weather can be temperamental. May to September is when most people prefer to visit; the summer weather is similar to that in southern Britain, though with more hours of sunshine and less rain. Stockholm can be a lovely autumnal city that still gets a fair amount of daylight between September and November, though it can also be grey and drizzly. The temperature starts to drop in October and it's not unheard of for snow to fall, though it doesn't generally settle. By November, the ground is usually covered in a blanket of snow, which will last until the following March or even April. Few could deny the enchanting beauty of the city at this time, when the city is awash with cosy Christmas markets and twinkly lights, and the bays, channels and canals freeze over, allowing Stockholmers to walk, ski and skate over the waterways and inlets of the sea.

Stockholm has, at various points in its history, been a significant cultural centre and key trading hub. Steam trains and freight trains, merchants and nobility have all passed through this city, leaving their mark in one way or another. Today, the city is not only the seat of Riksdagshuset (the national parliament), Kungliga Slottet (the Royal Palace) and many other places of historical interest, but is also the country's financial and business hub; over one-sixth of the total population of Sweden calls the Stockholm area home.

Culturally, Stockholm is thriving as never before, especially in the performing arts, which receive large government subsidies. The public purse supports the internationally acclaimed two hundred-year-old Kungliga Operan (Royal Opera), as well as the excellent Kungliga Dramatiska Teatern (Royal Dramatic Theatre). The city also boasts over eighty museums and a clutch of galleries. At one time nightlife was almost non-existent in Stockholm, but an explosion of nightclubs, trendy bars, contemporary restaurants and clubs has boosted the after-dark options here considerably.

This is an affluent city. Stockholmers live and dress well, and in the shops you'll find plenty of the clean, no-nonsense designer goods that have put Swedish design on the world stage. Once a relatively homogenous society, recent waves of immigration have brought a certain cultural diversity to the city. This is reflected in restaurant menus, with various international cuisines taking their place alongside the traditional Swedish options. You'll be spoilt for choice when choosing where to eat out in Stockholm, the city having been awarded the title of European Capital of Gastronomy in 2023; but wherever you go, you are guaranteed a culinary experience unlike any you've had before.

One could generalise about Stockholmers themselves by saying that they are a very pragmatic, orderly and reserved people with a strong sense of social consciousness and a progressive attitude to social welfare. Indeed, some of Sweden's

Royal Guard at the Palace

more innovative laws are revered the world over. The Swedes also remain close to nature; it is partly for this reason that as a summer city, Stockholm and its environs are hard to beat. There is music and dancing in the city parks, concerts at the Royal Palace, and recital music drifts from many of the museums and churches. At this time, the city's graceful silhouette is bathed in the eerily beautiful midsummer light, with plenty of opportunities for al fresco dining and outdoor swimming as everyone makes the most of the long hours of daylight.

What's new

VRAK – Museum of Wrecks (see page 55) opened on Djurgärden in 2021, along with a second building that was added to Liljevalchs Konsthall (see page 55). In 2022, the Avicii Experience (see page 35) launched in Norrmalm, while 2023 was a jubilee year in Sweden for many reasons: it celebrated five hundred years of Vasa reign, as well as marking the fiftieth year on the throne for the current King of Sweden – Carl XVI Gustaf. A series of exhibitions at the Royal Palace (see page 28) to mark this will spill over into the coming years. 2023 was also the 10th anniversary of the ABBA: The Museum (see page 56), celebrated with an ABBA Voyage exhibition that shows exclusive interviews and live footage; it's temporary but will remain in situ until at least 2025. Looking ahead, Stockholm Pride week in August 2024 is bound to be bigger than ever as Sweden celebrates eighty years since the decriminalisation of homosexuality and fifteen years of equal marriage, and in May 2025 Stockholm is due to co-host the Ice Hockey World Cup.

Where to...

Shop

Shopping in Sweden is a delightful entry into the world of design, and the capital offers a broad range of shops, boutiques and department stores. If you're looking for upmarket shops, you should head for Grev Turegatan, Biblioteksgatan, Birger Jarlsgatan and Norrmalmstorg in Östermalm. Here you'll find exclusive international labels alongside talented local designers. For fun shopping in a medieval milieu, try exploring Gamla Stan; Västerlånggatan, the pedestrian street bisecting the island, and the lanes surrounding it are lined with shops, boutiques and restaurants. Stockholm's main markets are the colourful Östermalmshallen, an indoor market noted for its cheese and fish specialities, and Hötorgshallen, a lively outdoor market where the locals buy their food from Monday to Saturday and shop for books, crafts and bric-a-brac. The district of Södermalm has trendy design shops, as well as antiques and second-hand shops, particularly around Götgatan, Hornsgatan and Folkungagatan streets.
OUR FAVOURITES: Östermalmshallen see page 83, NK see page 41, The English Bookshop see page 75.

Eat

Stockholm offers a great variety of dining establishments, and eating out here is a real pleasure. Recent years have brought pizzerias, burger chains and international restaurants to the capital, but there's still no dearth of genuine, old-fashioned Swedish food. Based largely around fish, meat and potatoes, traditional dishes are always well-presented and delicious; think marinated herring, meatballs, cloudberries, and cinnamon buns. Look for restaurants serving traditional Swedish dishes, such as *Janssons frestelse* (Jansson's Temptation), a delicious casserole of potatoes, anchovies, onion and cream; *pytt i panna* (diced meat, onions and potatoes); *strömming* (fried, boned herring from the Baltic Sea); or *köttbullar*, the world-famous Swedish meatballs. There are many inexpensive self-service cafeterias throughout the city, and most restaurants have small portions for kids at reduced prices.
OUR FAVOURITES: The Hills see page 78, Hasselbacken see page 60, Mälarpaviljongen see page 50.

Drink

Beer is the most common alcoholic drink in Sweden; it counts for roughly a third of all alcohol sold in Sweden. It's worth trying aquavit or schnapps, which is made from potatoes, served ice-cold in tiny shots and washed down with beer. It comes in dozens of weird and wonderful flavours, from lemon to cumin and dill. If you're visiting at Christmas, don't go home without having sampled *glögg*: mulled red wine with cloves, cinnamon, sugar and more than a shot of aquavit. Stockholmers like a drink and a dance, but there isn't a massive drinking culture here, and getting drunk is frowned upon; coffee, however, is very popular. In fact, at 3.2 cups per day on average, Swedes are the second biggest coffee-drinkers in the world, just behind the Finns.
OUR FAVOURITES: A Bar Called Gemma see page 91, Chewie's see page 51, Chokladkoppen see page 32.

Stockholm at a glance

Norrmalm p.34.
To the north of Gamla Stan, the district of Norrmalm swaps tradition for a thoroughly contemporary feel: this is Stockholm's downtown area, where you'll find shopping malls, huge department stores and conspicuous, showy wealth. The Central Station and the lively park known as Kungsträdgården are located here too.

Gamla Stan p.24.
The first stop for most visitors, Stockholm's Old Town is a medieval jumble of cobbled streets and narrow alleyways huddled together on a triangular-shaped island. A stroll along its meandering cobbled lanes is to take a trip back to in time.

Kungsholmen p.44.
Across the water from the uber-trendy Södermalm, Kungsholmen is a residential island that's fast becoming a rival to its southern neighbour for trendy restaurants, vintage shops and drinking establishments. It's also a hotspot for outdoor swimming and al fresco dining in the summer months.

Södermalm p.70.
The island of Södermalm was traditionally the working-class area of Stockholm but is now a haven for hipsters. Its grids of streets, lined with lofty stone buildings, create a homely ambience; it's here, in a fashionable area known as SoFo, that you'll find some of the city's most enjoyable bars and restaurants.

Observatorielunden

NORRMALM

Kronobergsparken

KUNGSHOLMEN

Riddarfjärden

Långholmsparken

LÅNGHOLMEN

Högalidsparken

Drakenbergsparken

Tantolunden

Eriksdalslunden

Östermalm p.82.

The more residential but very up-market area of Östermalm is pleasing mixture of grand avenues and smart houses, stately apartment buildings and foreign embassies. It's ideal for a spot of window-shopping in the pricey boutiques.

ÖSTERMALM

Ladugårdsgärdet

Historiska Museet

Sjöhistorska Museet
Museiparken

Nobelparken

Nybroviken

Ladugårdslandsviken

Djurgårdsbrunnsviken

Rosendals slott

Nationalmuseum

SKEPPSHOLMEN

Vasamuseet

Nordiska Museet

DJURGÅRDEN

Spiritmuseum

Moderna Museet

Arkitektur och Designcentrum (ArkDes)

Viking Museum
VRAK – Museum of Wrecks

Skansen

Liljevalchs Konsthall

ABBA: The Museum

Strommen

Gröna Lund

Beckholmen

Waldemarsviken

Prins Eugens Waldemarsudde

nhissen

Fotografiska

Djurgården p.52.

The leafy park island of Djurgården is the location of tons of museums and galleries, including the extraordinary seventeenth-century warship, Vasa, rescued and preserved after sinking in Stockholm harbour, and Skansen, the oldest and best of Europe's open-air museums.

Katarina kyrka

ÖDERMALM

Vitabergsparken

HENRIKSDAL

Hammarby sjö

Danviks kanalen

Sickla kanal

Sickla park

lasieholmen & Skeppsholmen p.62.

e tiny, peaceful island of Skeppsholmen is home to the
y's main modern art gallery and a quirky floating youth
stel. It's a green enclave in the middle of the city and a
ely place to take a relaxing stroll along the waterfront,
ile Blasieholmen is home to a number of elegant
laces as well as to the Nationalmuseet.

15

Things not to miss

It's not possible to see everything that Stockholm has to offer in one trip – and we don't suggest you try. What follows is a selective taste of the city's highlights, from a stunningly preserved warship to swimming at the city's best beach.

< **Kungliga Slottet**
See page 28
Learn about Sweden's much-loved royal family, and try to catch the famous changing of the guard.

∨ **Nationalmuseum**
See page 62
Wander around the stunning collection of paintings, sculptures and the like at Sweden's largest collection of art.

< **Skansen**
See page 57
Step into Sweden's past at the world's first, biggest and best open-air museum.

∨ **Stadshuset**
See page 44
Gaze in wonder at the eighteen million sparkling tiles that make up the mosaiced walls of the Golden Hall.

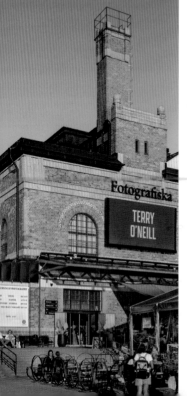

∧ **Moderna Museet**
See page 65
This striking building houses one of the finest collections of modern art in the world and should not be missed.

< **Fotografiska**
See page 70
World-renowned contemporary photography abounds at this small but fascinating gallery, within a former customs house.

∧ Kungsträdgården
See page 38
Stockholm's most popular
hangout is always buzzing, with
open-air concerts in summer and
an ice rink during winter.

∨ Gamla Stan
See page 29
The crowded, compact, cobbled
streets of the Old Town are ripe
for exploration; take a walking
tour, or simply let yourself get lost.

∧ **Underground art tour**
See page 35
Ride Stockholm's metro, known as the *tunnelbana* or T-bana, and discover the world's largest free art gallery; many of its one hundred stations are filled with artwork.

< **Drottningholm Palace**
See page 97
The private residence of the Swedish royal family is partly open to the public, and has been described as the Versailles of Sweden.

< **Swimming at Smedsuddsbadet**
See page 48
Make like the Swedes and stop off at this sandy city beach for a walk, run, cycle, swim or barbecue.

∨ **Östermalmshallen**
See page 83
Lose yourself in this late nineteenth-century food hall among stalls selling seafood, cheese, antiques, coffee, and other treasures.

Day One in Stockholm

Kungliga Slottet See page 28. Start your day with a tour of the Royal Palace, taking in the beautifully preserved Rococo interior of the Royal Chapel and Queen Christina's silver throne in the Hall of State.

Gamla Stan See page 29. From here, take a walking tour of the history-filled streets and medieval cobbled alleyways of Stockholm's Old Town.

Fika at Chokladkoppen See page 32. Grab the customary coffee and cake at queer-run Chokladkoppen, known for making the biggest cinnamon buns in town.

Kungliga Slottet

🍴 **Lunch at Hotel Skeppsholmen** See page 68. Take the ferry to the idyllic island of Skeppsholmen and stop off at this quaint house that once served as Royal Marine barracks, but is now a hotel that serves delicious meatballs.

Moderna Museet See page 65. Spend the afternoon at one of the best modern art collections Europe has to offer, with works by such masters as Miró, Matisse, and Modigliani.

Moderna Museet

Nationalmuseum See page 62. Cross the iconic Skeppsholmsbron to get to the Nationalmuseum, which contains the largest collection of art in Scandinavia; it reopened in 2018 after a huge, five-year, £100-million refurbishment.

🍴 **Dinner at The Veranda** See page 69. After a long day of sightseeing, treat yourself to a famous Swedish smörgåsbord and a small bottle of aquavit at this delightful restaurant in the Grand Hôtel.

Smörgåsbord at the Grand Hotel

Day Two in Stockholm

Stockholms Stadshus See page 44. Begin the day by gazing in awe at the eighteen million sparkling tiles that cover the walls in the Golden Hall, and wondering at the gorgeous Blue Hall (which is actually red).

Fotografiska See page 70. Take public transport to Fotografiska; one of the world's biggest galleries for modern photography is housed in a striking red-brick building that used to be a customs warehouse.

Stadshus

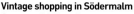

🍽 **Lunch at Barabao** See page 77. Wander through Stockholm's trendiest district, taking in stunning harbour views, before making a swift stop for a soft steamed bao bun or four at this trendy restaurant full of hanging plants.

Vintage shopping in Södermalm See page 74. From here, you can walk the length of Hornsgatan, a road littered with hip vintage boutiques and shops full of second-hand treasures.

🍸 **Cocktail at Hellstens Glashus** See page 80. Double back on yourself for a refreshing pre-dinner cocktail at the industrial-chic bar at Hellstens Glashus.

Shopping on Södermalm

🍽 **Dinner at The Hills** See page 78. Have dinner at this trendy Stockholm hotspot to recharge your batteries after a day of walking – try not to jump when you spot the blank-faced mannequin by the toilets!

Dancing at Debaser See page 81. Hop in a cab and spend the night dancing at one of Debaser's buzzy events. Equally, if you're visiting in summer, this would be a great time to head to the nearby island of Långholmen for a post-dinner dip.

Långholmen swimmers

Stockholm Museums

Stockholm is home to world-class, unique and wide-ranging museums; several of them are rather helpfully placed close together on the leafy park island of Djurgården.

Nordiska Museet See page 52. Discover the last five hundred years of Sweden's history at the palatial Nordiska Museet, with over one million objects displayed.

Vasamuseet See page 52. Close by is the Vasamuseet. If you only go to one museum in Stockholm, make it this one: it is the permanent home of the perfectly preserved seventeenth-century warship that lay at the bottom of the Stockholm harbour for over three hundred years, until it was brought to the surface in 1961.

🍽 **Lunch at Hasselbacken** See page 60. Stop at this beautifully designed restaurant for lunch, also the birthplace of the famous Hasselback potato.

ABBA: The Museum See page 56. A light-hearted jaunt around the ABBA Museum is sure to put a smile on the faces of superfans and casual observers alike. Remember to pick up the red phone if it rings – it's a member of ABBA on the other line. Ring ring!

Skansen See page 57. The world's first and largest open-air museum includes tons of history as well as a zoo, an aquarium, and a whole host of craft-makers. Don't forget to grab a scrumptious cinnamon bun.

🍽 **Dinner and a show at Cirkus** See page 60. For the perfect end to a perfect day, have dinner at the first-class restaurant of this historic nineteenth-century events venue, and try to catch one of their wide-ranging shows or spectacles.

Nordiska Museet

Hasselbacken

Skansen

The Stockholm Archipelago

Some thirty thousand islands dot the Baltic Sea to form the Stockholm Archipelago – a boat trip from the city guarantees an awe-inspiring day out.

Artipelag See page 93. Catch a boat to Artipelag, a distinctive complex that focuses on art, architecture, and food, and spend the morning wandering around colourful art exhibits or getting lost in the forest on their various nature walks. Don't miss a stop at Bådan Café for fika by pastry chef Annie Hesselstad, known for creating the dessert at 2022's Nobel Banquet.

Lunch at Smådalarö Gård See page 113. Jump back on the boat and enjoy the scenery as you make your way to the island of Dalarö and one of Sweden's most chic countryside spa hotels, Smådalarö Gård. Enjoy a lunch of locally sourced ingredients at the restaurant when you arrive.

Wood-fired sauna and coldwater swim See page 110. There are plenty of activities to enjoy in the archipelago – kayaking and stand-up paddleboarding are very popular – but no trip to Sweden would be complete without a Swedish sauna ritual, which involves spending time getting sweaty in the sauna before jumping into the cold waters of the Baltic.

Fjäderholmarna See page 95. Jump back on the boat and head to Stockholm's closest archipelago islands for a wander around the handicraft village of independent shops and artists' studios.

Dinner at Rökeriet See page 96. Enjoy a tasty seafood dinner at Rökeriet, a friendly fish smokery on Fjäderholmarna overlooking the water, before heading back to the city at sunset.

Sculpture on Artipelag

Sauna in the archipelago

Fjäderholmarna

PLACES

Östermalm harbour

Gamla Stan

Gamla Stan is the oldest – and arguably the most beautiful – part of Stockholm. Three islands – Riddarholmen, Staden and Helgeandsholmen – make up the Old Town, which comprises a cluster of seventeenth- and eighteenth-century buildings backed by hairline medieval alleys. It was on these three adjoining islands that Birger Jarl erected the town's first fortifications in the thirteenth century, meaning that this is the place where Stockholm was originally founded. It's not surprising, then, that much of Stockholm's history is concentrated in Gamla Stan's cobbled lanes, winding alleys, mansions, palaces and soaring spires. Strictly speaking, only the largest island, Staden, contains Gamla Stan; but the name is commonly attached to the buildings and streets of all three islands.

Riddarholmskyrkan

MAP PAGE 26, POCKET MAP B12–13
Riddarholmen Church. Birger Jarls Torg 3, Gamla Stan T-bana, Ⓦ kungligaslotten. se/english/royal-palaces-and-sites/the-riddarholmen-church.html, charge.

It's only a matter of seconds to cross the bridge from the Riddarhuset via the nearby bridge, Riddarholmsbron, onto the non-residential island of Riddarholmen (Nobility Island), and thus to

Sweden's queer Queen?

Ascending to the Swedish throne in 1632 aged just six, Queen Christina of Sweden is an almost mythical figure of royal history that scholars have been arguing over for centuries; depictions range from a headstrong troublemaker to an ardent feminist four hundred years ahead of her time. In reality, she was likely to have been a bit of both. Christina abdicated the throne at the age of 27, citing her reasons as a sense of revulsion towards the idea of marriage, an unwillingness to convert from Catholicism to the Lutheran church, and an aversion to the pressures of her royal role. She spent the next part of her life plotting (unsuccessfully) to steal the crowns of no less than three different kingdoms. Stories of her behaviour during this time are rousing and chaotic, including having a French Marquis beheaded for betraying her plot to become the Queen of Naples. Christina also raised eyebrows with her gender expression and sexuality; she reportedly "walked like a man, sat and rode like a man, and could eat and swear like the roughest soldiers", routinely shocking the courts she visited. Christina's self-described "bed-fellow" Countess Ebba Sparre, with whom she shared "a long-time intimate companionship", was also a source of repeated controversy.

Gamla Stan

Riddarholmskyrkan. Originally a Franciscan monastery, the church has been the burial place of Swedish royalty for over six centuries; all rulers of Sweden since Gustav II Adolf have been buried here, with the exception of Queen Christina (see page 24). Important people who visit Stockholm also get a plaque that is moved inside this building when they pass away; you can find Mahatma Gandhi inside, and Barack Obama will also get one when he dies.

The interior is a pleasing mix of simplicity and regality, and the walls are covered in the coats of arms of the Knights of the Seraphim Order. The floor is littered with about two hundred graves. The last regular service was held here in 1807; these days it is only used for memorial and burial services.

Walk around the back of the church to Riddarholmen quay for stunning views of Lake Mälaren, the heights of Söder (southern Stockholm) and Stadshuset on Kungsholmen, which appears as though it is rising straight out of Lake Mälaren. Face out west from Gamla Stan, and the water you're looking at is the same freshwater that you'll also find running from Stockholm's taps; if you were to look to the east of the Old Town, you'd see the salt waters of the Baltic Sea. In summer, this spot is a gorgeous place for swimming and a sundowner by the water – it's facing west so has a romantic view of the sunset; in winter, the lake can freeze from here right as far as the Västerbron bridge, a couple of kilometres further west, and people skate and take their dogs for walks along the ice.

Riddarhuset

MAP PAGE 26, POCKET MAP C12

House of the Nobility. Riddarhustorget 10, Gamla Stan T-bana, Ⓦ riddarhuset.se, charge.

On the north side of a square called Riddarhustorget is Riddarhuset, a handsome, seventeenth-century Baroque building known in English as the House of the Nobility that some argue is Stockholm's most beautiful building. The original architect, a Frenchman named Vallée, was stabbed to death in a dispute over the building plans, but his son went on to complete the redbrick and sandstone structure in

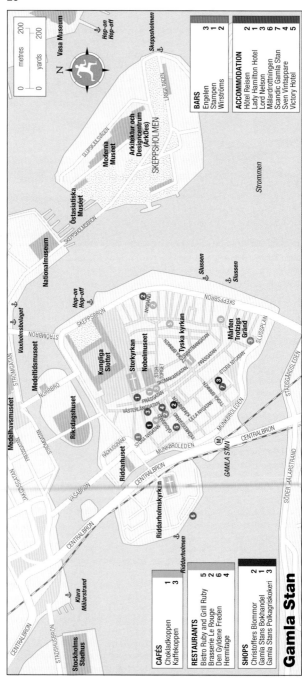

Gamla Stan

BARS
Engelen	3
Stampen	1
Wirströms	2

ACCOMMODATION
Hôtel Reisen	2
Lady Hamilton Hotel	1
Lord Nelson	3
Mälardrottningen	6
Scandic Gamla Stan	7
Sven Vintappare	4
Victory Hotel	5

CAFÉS
Chokladkoppen	1
Kaffekoppen	3

RESTAURANTS
Bistro Ruby and Grill Ruby	5
Brasserie Le Rouge	2
Den Gyldene Freden	6
Hermitage	4

SHOPS
Christoffers Blommor	2
Gamla Stans Bokhandel	1
Gamla Stans Polkagriskokeri	3

1660 with the help of a dedicated team. Its Great Hall was used by the Swedish aristocracy for two hundred years for parliamentary debate until a law was passed in 1865 to create Sweden's current two-chamber parliament. The coats of arms of Sweden's six hundred-odd noble families – around two-and-a-half-thousand of them – are splattered across the walls; these days, the nobility doesn't have any special societal privileges to speak of, but they can still use this house for weddings and parties. Take a peek at the Chancery downstairs, which stores heraldic bone china by the shelf-load and has racks full of fancy signet rings – essential accessories for the eighteenth-century noble-about-town. The Riddarhuset is due to reopen in late 2024, following extensive renovation.

Riksdagshuset

MAP PAGE 26, POCKET MAP C12
Parliament building. Riksgatan 1, Gamla Stan T-bana, ⓦ riksdagen.se, free.
The Riksdagshuset is the Swedish Parliament building, and is open to anyone who would like to attend a debate or public hearing. It is

here that Sweden's famous welfare state was shaped during the 1940s and 1950s. The building was completely restored in the 1970s, just seventy years after it was built, and the original, columned facade is rarely used as an entrance today; the main entrance is on Riksgatan, the short street between the bridges of Riksbron and Stallbron. It's the glassy bulge at the back that is the hub of most activity, and where you're shown around on the free guided tours that run on the weekends when parliament is in session (advance booking is required). The seating for the 349 members is in healthy, non-adversarial rows, grouped by constituency and not by party, and nobody bats an eyelid if politicians breastfeed their babies in the chamber.

Medeltidsmuseet

MAP PAGE 26, POCKET MAP C11
Museum of Medieval Stockholm. Strömparterren 3, T-Centralen T-bana, ⓦ medeltidsmuseet.stockholm, free.
In front of the Riksdagshuset, a small set of steps leads down to a park, Strömparterren, home to the

Riddarhuset

Medeltidsmuseet, the Medieval Museum of Stockholm. Inside you'll find medieval ruins, tunnels and parts of Stockholm's city walls dating from the 1530s, which were discovered during excavations under the parliament building and have been incorporated into a walk-through underground exhibition. Reconstructed houses of timber and brick, complete with wax models peering out of the windows, help give a realistic idea of what life was like in sixteenth-century Stockholm. However, it's the extensive remains of the 20m-long Riddarholm ship, dating from the early 1520s, which really draws the eye. Built in overlapping clinker style, common during Viking times, the ship had been equipped with cannons and lead shot before sinking in the Riddarholm canal in the 1520s.

Kungliga Slottet

MAP PAGE 26, POCKET MAP C12
Royal Palace. Slottsbacken, Gamla Stan
T-bana, ⓦ kungahuset.se, charge.

Perhaps the most monumental building in Stockholm, the Kungliga Slottet or Royal Palace is the official residence of His Majesty the King and UNESCO World Heritage Site with over six hundred rooms. Until the present monarch, Carl XVI Gustaf, decided to reside at Drottningholm, it was one of the biggest palaces in the world to be inhabited by royalty. The palace itself is a squat, square, brown construction, with two arms that stretch down towards the water. Traditionally, these two arms held separate apartments for the King and Queen, the Queen's side being the one with the better view of the water. It was here in the King's royal bedchamber that King Gustav III died after being shot at the Royal Opera house; his deathbed had an unfortunate view over the building in which he was mortally wounded. The apartments have also played host to the late Swedish DJ Avicii, who played a private set here for Prince Carl Philip and Sofia Hellqvist's wedding in 2015.

Stockholm's old Tre Kronor (Three Crowns) castle burnt down at the beginning of King Karl XII's reign (1697–1718), allowing his architect to design a simple and beautiful Baroque structure in its stead. Finished in 1754, the palace

Karl XI Gallery in the Royal Palace

Gamla Stan streets

is a striking achievement: uniform and sombre outside, but with a magnificent Rococo interior that's a swirl of staterooms and museums.

Kungliga Slottet is remarkably accessible to the public, although parts, or all, may be closed for affairs of state; its sheer size is quite overwhelming and it's worth focusing your explorations on one or two sections of the palace. Be sure not to miss the beautifully preserved Rococo interior of the Royal Chapel and Queen Christina's silver throne in the Hall of State, as well as the Apartments of the Orders of Chivalry, which houses a permanent collection of the regal orders.

The changing of the guard takes place here every day, at 12.15pm during the week and at 1.15pm on Sundays. It's a real spectacle and a lot of fun if you have the chance to see it; there's much pomp and circumstance surrounding the event, and the whole charade takes around forty minutes to complete.

Gamla Stan streets

South of Kungliga Slottet, the streets suddenly narrow and you're into Gamla Stan proper. The best

way to get the feel of the Old Town is to wander its maze of stone streets at will. There's something to experience at every turn – antiques, shops housed in fine fifteenth and sixteenth-century buildings, former merchant palaces, gabled houses decorated with ornate portals and delightful alleyways with names like Gåsgränd (Goose Lane) and Skeppar Karls Gränd (Skipper Karl's Lane). You'll also come across art shops, galleries and smart boutiques selling clothes, handcrafted jewellery and ceramics and plenty of cosy cafés serving decent coffee and kanelbulle (cinnamon rolls). Crime is not common in Sweden, but pickpockets do roam these areas, taking advantage of the crowded streets and distracted tourists – so keep a close eye on your bags to be on the safe side.

Storkyrkan

MAP PAGE 26, POCKET MAP C12
Great Church. Trångsund 1, Gamla Stan T-bana, Ⓦ stockholmmuseums.se/en/museum/Storkyrkan, charge; free for under 18s.

The highest point of the old part of Stockholm is crowned by the

Storkyrkan, built in 1279, and almost the first building you'll stumble upon. Pedantically speaking, Stockholm has no cathedral, but this rectangular brick church is now accepted as such, and the monarchs of Sweden married and were crowned here. The Storkyrkan dates from the thirteenth century, but gained its present shape at the end of the fifteenth century following a series of earlier alterations and additions; it was given a Baroque remodelling in the 1730s to better fit in with the new palace taking shape next door. The somewhat dull exterior gives no hint at the beauty of the marvellous Gothic interior: twentieth-century restoration removed the white plaster from its redbrick columns, giving a warm colouring to the rest of the building. Much is made of the fifteenth-century Gothic sculpture of St George and the Dragon, which symbolizes Sweden's struggles to break free of Denmark and is certainly an animated piece, though easily overshadowed by the royal pews – more like golden billowing thrones – and the monumental black-and-silver altarpiece.

Stortorget

MAP PAGE 26, POCKET MAP C12

Stortorget (or Great Square) is Gamla Stan's main square, one block south of the Storkyrkan along either Trångsund or Källargränd. It's a handsome and elegantly proportioned space crowded with eighteenth-century buildings. But the cheerfully coloured buildings, water features and flowers here give no hint of the square's murderous history; in 1520, Christian II of Denmark used it as an execution site during the so-called 'Stockholm Bloodbath', dispatching his opposition with bloody finality when he ordered the beheading of some eighty Swedish noblemen, left their bodies to bleed out, and piled their heads pyramid-style in the middle of the square. It began raining hard, which washed the blood from the square until the whole town was running with rivulets of red blood – and it's from here that we get the term 'bloodbath'. Nowadays, the square

Interior of Storkyrkan

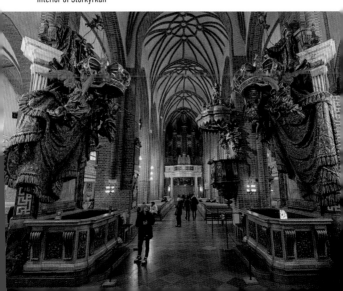

Stortorget

has quite a different vibe, and makes for a pretty spot to stop for coffee and people-watch. You can fill your water bottle up at the fountain in the centre, which spouts perfectly potable (and delicious) drinking water.

Nobelmuseet

MAP PAGE 26, POCKET MAP C12
Nobel Prize Museum. Stortorget 2, Ⓦ nobelprizemuseum.se, charge; free for under-19s.

Among the fine old houses on Stortorget is the Börsen, the former Stock Exchange, which is a handsome building dating from 1776. Members of the Swedish Academy meet here to elect the Nobel Prize winners in literature. The building is also home to the Nobelmuseet (Nobel Prize Museum), which uses cutting-edge design and technology to document the history and the world of the Nobel Prize – specifically, Alfred Nobel himself and the more than seven hundred laureates. It's full of information – so expect to leave both informed and entertained.

Tyska kyrkan

MAP PAGE 26, POCKET MAP C12
German Church. Kindstugatan, Gamla Stan T-bana, Ⓦ svenskakyrkan.se/ deutschegemeinde, charge.

Once belonging to Stockholm's medieval German merchants, the Tyska kyrkan served as the meeting place of the Guild of St Gertrude. A copper-roofed red-brick building, it was enlarged in the seventeenth century when Baroque decorators got hold of it: the result, an opulent interior with the pulpit dominating the nave. The royal gallery in one corner adds to the overall elegance.

Mårten Trotzigs Gränd

MAP PAGE 26, POCKET MAP C13
Mårten Trotzigs Gränd is famous for being the narrowest street in Stockholm. It is named after Mårten Trotzig, a German merchant who emigrated to Stockholm in 1581, later to become one of the richest merchants in the city before meeting a sticky end in 1617. This steep, lamplit, stone stairway is just 90cm (25in) wide and takes you on to Prästgatan.

Shops

Christoffers Blommor

MAP PAGE 26, POCKET MAP C12
Kåkbrinken 10, Gamla Stan T-bana,
Ⓦ christoffersblommor.se.

Every morning, florist Christoffer
Broman transforms the narrow
alley outside his flower shop into
a lush oasis as he starts arranging
flowers and plants. A charming and
friendly little place, Christoffers
Blommor has a host of regular
locals who firmly claim it to be the
best in town.

Gamla Stans Bokhandel

MAP PAGE 26, POCKET MAP C12
Stora Nygatan 7, Gamla Stan T-bana,
Ⓦ gamlastansbokhandel.se.

A lovely bookshop on Stockholm's
oldest boulevard, Gamla Stans
Bokhandel is a little oasis of
calm amidst the crowds of the
Old Town. The shop has a
wide selection of hand-picked
bestsellers in Swedish and English
and the staff are exceptionally
helpful. They regularly host

Chokladkoppen

well-attended talks, readings and
book signings.

Gamla Stans Polkagriskokeri

MAP PAGE 26, POCKET MAP C13
Stora Nygatan 44, Gamla Stan T-bana,
Ⓦ gamlastanspolkagriskokeri.se.

A must for those with a sweet
tooth, this gorgeous sweetshop
hand-makes polkagrisar, a
traditional Swedish peppermint-
flavoured hard candy; you can even
see it being made in the kitchen as
you browse! Nowadays there are
lots of flavours to choose from,
and even some chocolate too. Keep
your eyes peeled for free samples!

Cafés

Chokladkoppen

MAP PAGE 26, POCKET MAP C12
Stortorget 18, Gamla Stan T-bana,
Ⓦ chokladkoppen.se.

A fabulous, cosy café overlooking
Gamla Stan's main square,
specialising in white chocolate
cheesecake and blueberry pie,
and famous for its legendary
cinnamon buns and hot chocolate;
it also serves tasty salmon quiches
and light lunch dishes. This is a
proudly queer-run place, and was
the first place in Stockholm to fly
the rainbow flag in 1997; it's still
cheerfully decked out in them
today. Kr

Kaffekoppen

MAP PAGE 26, POCKET MAP C12
Stortorget 20, Gamla Stan T-bana,
Ⓦ cafekaffekoppen.se.

Immediately next door to
Chokladkoppen, Kaffekoppen
(the former means 'chocolate
cup' and the latter 'coffee cup')
is another classic café in Gamla
Stan, having been open on
Stortorget since 1994. The café
is in a rustic, exposed brick wall
basement, and the pastries are to
die for – they also tend to be huge
and very reasonably priced. Kr

Restaurants

Bistro Ruby and Grill Ruby

MAP PAGE 26, POCKET MAP D12
Österlånggatan 14, Gamla Stan T-bana,
Ⓦ grillruby.com.

Bistro Ruby is an intimate, long-established French place, romantically done up in Parisian style with red walls covered with artwork. Next door, though in the same building, is Grill Ruby, which serves up TexMex and American-style charcoal grills of meat and fish and weekend brunches. KrKrKr

Brasserie Le Rouge

MAP PAGE 26, POCKET MAP D12
Brunnsgränd 2–4, Gamla Stan T-bana,
Ⓦ instagram.com/lerougesthlm.

A gloriously OTT Moulin Rouge-style bistro, inspired by nineteenth-century Paris, where everything from the drapes to the sofas are de rigueur bright red. Especially good are the pan-fried Icelandic salmon and Scottish highland steak. With impeccable service and candlelit tables, this place is one of the most ostentatiously romantic there is. KrKrKr

Den Gyldene Freden

MAP PAGE 26, POCKET MAP D13
Österlånggatan 51, Gamla Stan T-bana,
Ⓦ gyldenefreden.se.

Opened in 1722, Stockholm's oldest and now most famous and prestigious restaurant is housed in a combination of vaulted brick cellars and regular serving rooms that are pure eighteenth century. Its name, which means 'the Golden Peace', comes from the peace treaty made with Russia in 1721. Serving delicious traditional Swedish cuisine (think pikeperch and meatballs), superb service, and a fabulous atmosphere, a night out here isn't quite as pricey as you might expect, given its reputation. KrKrKr

Hermitage

MAP PAGE 26, POCKET MAP C12
Stora Nygatan 11, Gamla Stan T-bana,
Ⓣ 08 411 95 00.

Hermitage is a long-established and well-respected vegetarian restaurant whose menu often features a few Middle Eastern dishes. You can get a great buffet lunch here, as well as a very reasonable set dinner menu; come for the delicious food and delightful vibes. Kr

Bars

Engelen

MAP PAGE 26, POCKET MAP C13
Kornhamnstorg 59, Gamla Stan T-bana,
Ⓦ engelen.se.

A great place to see cover bands who perform most nights in various guises: jazz, rock or blues. Engelen has a large and loyal clientele, so arrive early to get in. There's also a dance floor downstairs.

Stampen

MAP PAGE 26, POCKET MAP C12
Stora Nygatan 5, Gamla Stan T-bana,
Ⓦ stampen.se.

Rowdy jazz club, which is best known for swing, dixie and trad, though there's mainstream, blues and 1950s and 1960s rock, too. Stampen has been cranking out live music most nights for the past forty years and is still going strong.

Wirströms

MAP PAGE 26, POCKET MAP C12
Stora Nygatan 13, Gamla Stan T-bana,
Ⓦ wirstromspub.se.

A great favourite among Stockholm's expat community who come to this authentic Irish pub to talk football and sample the large selection of beers and whiskies. There are also a few bar meals such as fish and chips and burgers, as well as live music, quiz nights and disco bingo.

Norrmalm

To the north of the Old Town, the district of Norrmalm, with its glass and steel skyscrapers, malls, underpasses and roundabouts, has both feet planted firmly in the late twentieth century. This is the compact heart of modern Stockholm, where you'll find shopping malls and department stores, offices, bars, cinemas, restaurants and conspicuous, showy wealth. The Central Station and the lively park known as Kungsträdgården are located here too.

Sergels Torg

MAP PAGE 36, POCKET MAP B11
Sergel Square. T-Centralen T-bana.
Stockholm's equivalent of Trafalgar Square, or Times Square, is found at the bilevel Sergels Torg, which has become the focal point of the modern city. Named after Johan Tobias Sergel, an eighteenth-century court sculptor, it is the centre of the city's shopping district with traffic circling around a huge glass obelisk that sits in the centre of a fountain, and an open-air pedestrian precinct on

Sergels Torg

the lower level. The market stalls, protesters and street entertainers here attract lots of shoppers and curious onlookers.

Kulturhuset

MAP PAGE 36, POCKET MAP C11
House of Culture. Sergels torg 3, T-Centralen T-bana, ⓦ kulturhusetstadsteatern.se, free; charge for exhibitions.
The dominant building of Sergels Torg is the huge, glass fronted Kulturhuset, devoted to contemporary Swedish culture. Hundreds of people flock here daily to see art and handicraft exhibitions, watch films, listen to music, poetry and dramatic readings, or enjoy a fine view over the city while drinking coffee at the Café Panorama. Those with children should make a beeline for the fourth floor, where there are three 'book' rooms, complete with hammocks and hideaways. The Stockholm Stadsteater (Municipal Theatre), which stages modern and classical plays in Swedish, is also here.

Klara kyrka

MAP PAGE 36, POCKET MAP B11
Church of Saint Clare. Klara Östra Kyrkogatan 7, T-Centralen T-bana, free.
Hemmed in on all sides, with only its spires visible from the streets around, Klara kyrka is particularly delicate church. It has a light and

Underground art

The Stockholm subway (known in Swedish as the tunnelbana, or T-bana) is one of the world's longest subway systems. Just over 39 miles (63km) of its total length of 67 miles (109km), are actually underground, as are around half of its 100 stations. But its most famous claim to fame is that it is the longest free art gallery in the world; around ninety per cent of its stations feature some kind of public artwork. From its inception, the tunnelbana doubled as a venue for displaying the work of the city's most creative artists, and millions of kroner are set aside annually to help maintain the tradition, which has so far showcased some 140 artists. As a result, locals and tourists are treated to a succession of inventive paintings, murals, sculptures and mosaic works of art as they go about their daily commute. Some of the most beautiful stations are the blue patterns at Norrmalm's T-Centralen, the garden-themed sculptures, mosaics, fountains, and even old palace doors at Kungsträdgården, and the colourful rainbow mural at Östermalm's Stadion.

flowery eighteenth-century painted interior and an impressive golden pulpit; out in the churchyard, a memorial stone commemorates the eighteenth-century Swedish poet Carl Michael Bellman, whose popular, lengthy ballads are said to have been composed extempore; his unmarked grave is somewhere in the churchyard.

Avicii Experience

MAP PAGE 36, POCKET MAP B10-C10
Sergels Torg 2, -Centralen T-bana,
🌐 aviciiexperience.com, charge.

The Avicii Experience is one of Stockholm's newest offerings, having opened in 2022. The interactive museum is a tribute to the life of Tim 'Avicii' Bergling, the internationally known Swedish DJ sensation and Stockholm native who died by suicide in 2018. The experience does a brilliant job of making sure his legacy and work are well represented and respected; there's a lot of information about his life and music, including the huge significance of his 2011 single *Levels* which made him internationally famous at the age of 21. The input from his friends, family and co-workers

is particularly touching. Overall, though, the museum honours Avicii by focusing on the joy of music; there's the chance to hear unreleased tracks and VR opportunities to sing your heart out in front of thousands of screaming fans.

Hötorget

MAP PAGE 36, POCKET MAP B10
Hötorget T-bana.

Stockholm's main market square is the opulent, cobbled Hötorget. The Art Deco hotels make a scenic backdrop for the daily open-air fruit, vegetable and flower market, which runs from roughly 9am to 5pm even in winter; you'll also find the wonderful Hötorgshallen here, an indoor market boasting a tantalizing array of restaurants and takeaway food options. The tall hotel building across the square, PUB, is a former department store where Greta Garbo once worked (see page 38). Hötorget is also home to Stockholm's biggest cinema complex, the Filmstaden Sergel; to the east, Kungsgatan, running across to Stureplan and Birger Jarlsgatan, has most of the rest of the city's cinemas,

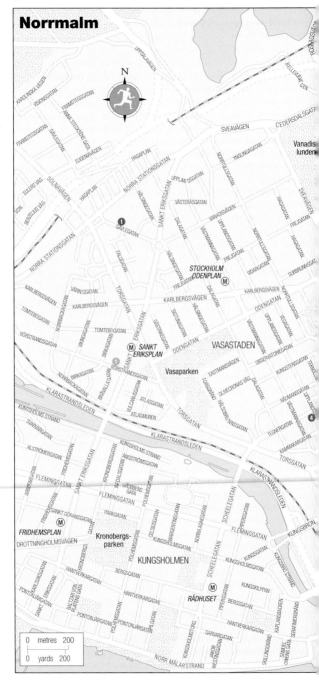

Norrmalm

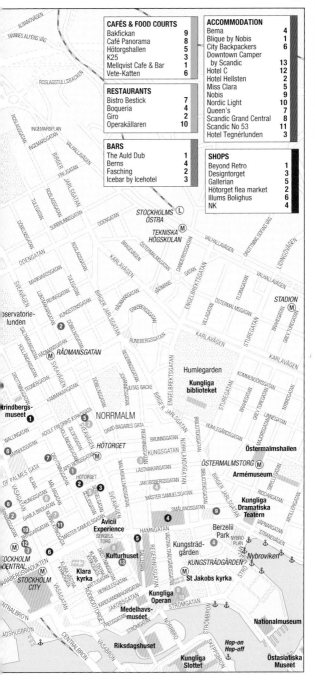

CAFÉS & FOOD COURTS

Bakfickan	9
Café Panorama	8
Hötorgshallen	5
K25	3
Mellqvist Cafe & Bar	1
Vete-Katten	6

RESTAURANTS

Bistro Bestick	7
Boqueria	4
Giro	2
Operakällaren	10

BARS

The Auld Dub	1
Berns	4
Fasching	2
Icebar by Icehotel	3

ACCOMMODATION

Bema	4
Blique by Nobis	1
City Backpackers	6
Downtown Camper by Scandic	13
Hotel C	12
Hotel Hellsten	2
Miss Clara	5
Nobis	9
Nordic Light	10
Queen's	7
Scandic Grand Central	8
Scandic No 53	11
Hotel Tegnérlunden	3

SHOPS

Beyond Retro	1
Designtorget	3
Gallerian	5
Hötorget flea market	2
Illums Bolighus	6
NK	4

Greta Garbo in Stockholm

Greta Garbo (1905–90) began her working life in Hötorget in Stockholm. She toiled as a sales assistant in the hat section of the PUB department store on the square before hitting the big time, acting in no fewer than 27 films. She spent most of her life in the United States, dying in New York in 1990, and it wasn't until 1999 that her ashes were returned to Stockholm after a long legal battle. Garbo is buried in the Skogskyrkogården cemetery in Enskede in the south of Stockholm (take the T-bana green line to the station called Skogskyrkogården to visit).

interspersed with agreeable little cafés and bars.

Drottninggatan
MAP PAGE 36, POCKET MAP C3, B10–C10
T-Centralen T-bana.
Another of Stockholm's main shopping streets, Drottninggatan is a long, mostly pedestrianised thoroughfare that is absolutely choc-a-bloc with all kinds of shops; expect small specialist boutiques alongside Swedish behemoths like H&M, Cos and Arket, as well as international chains including Zara. You'll also find vintage shops like Beyond Retro (see page 41) as well as tourist shops selling souvenirs, stalls selling hot doughnuts and the occasional street performer.

Strindbergsmuseet
MAP PAGE 36, POCKET MAP C3
Strindberg Museum. Drottninggatan 85, Rådmansgatan T-bana,
strindbergsmuseet.se, charge.
At the northern end of Drottninggatan, you'll come to the intriguing Strindbergsmuseet in the 'Blue Tower', the building in which the playwright August Strindberg lived during the last years of his life, between 1908 and 1912. The house is so carefully preserved that you must put plastic bags over your shoes on entering to protect the floors and furnishings. The study is a dark and gloomy place just as Strindberg left it on his death; he always wrote with the Venetian

blinds and heavy curtains closed against the sunlight. Upstairs, his library is a musty room with all the books firmly behind glass, which is a great shame as Strindberg was far from a passive reader. He underlined heavily and criticized in the margins as he read, though rather less eruditely than you'd expect – "Lies!", "Crap!", "Idiot!" and "Bloody hell!" tended to be his favourite comments.

Hamngatan
MAP PAGE 36, POCKET MAP C10
Kungsträdgården T-bana.
Leading east from Sergels Torg is Hamngatan, one of the main shopping streets. Its tenants include NK, Sweden's biggest department store (see page 41), alongside Gallerian, a mall with many shops and restaurants (see page 41). The previously public spaces of Sverigehuset (Sweden House) are now home to Illums Bolighus, a well-known Danish interior design shop (see page 41). The building was designed by one of the most important modernist Swedish architects, Sven Markelius (1889–1972). In fact, there are many instances of intriguing architecture on this street if you can bear to drag your eyes away from the enticing shop fronts; look out for the bottle green tiles of number 26.

Kungsträdgården
MAP PAGE 36, POCKET MAP C11
Kungsträdgården T-bana.

Norrmalm's eastern boundary is marked by the Kungsträdgården, the most fashionable and central of the city's numerous parks, reaching northwards from the water as far as Hamngatan. The mouthful of a name literally means 'the king's gardens', though if you're expecting perfectly designed flowerbeds and rose gardens you'll be disappointed – it's a pedestrianized paved square, albeit in the form of an elongated rectangle, with a couple of lines of elm and cherry trees, and its days as a royal kitchen garden are long gone. Today the area is Stockholm's main meeting place, especially in summer, when there's almost always something going on: free music, live theatre and other performances take place on the central open-air stage. There are also several popular cafés: the outdoors one off Strömgatan at Kungsträdgården's southern edge is popular in spring as a place for winter-weary Stockholmers to lap up the sunshine. In winter, the park is as busy as in summer: the Isbanan, an open-air ice rink at the Hamngatan end of the park, rents out skates.

St Jakobs kyrka

MAP PAGE 36, POCKET MAP C11
St Jakobs Church. Västra Trädgårdsgatan 2, Kungsträdgården T-bana, free.

Though located in a prime position opposite the opera house, seventeenth-century St Jakobs kyrka is often overlooked by visitors to the city. It stands on the site of an earlier chapel of St James (Jakob in Swedish) and was completed fifty years after the death of its founder, Johan III. Although the church's doors are impressive – check out the south door with its statues of Moses and St James on either side – it's the great, golden pulpit that draws most attention. The date of the building's completion (1642) is stamped high up on the ceiling in gold relief. Organ recitals are occasionally held here, usually on Fridays at 5pm. Nearby you'll find the small, attractive park of Karl XII's Torg, which is dominated by a statue of the king himself, Sweden's most celebrated historical figure.

Drottninggatan

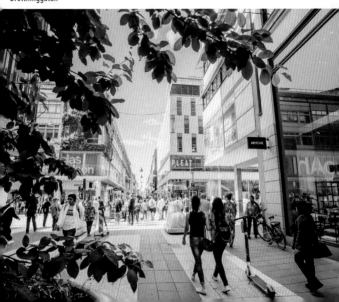

Kungliga Operan

MAP PAGE 36, POCKET MAP C11
Royal Opera House. Gustav Adolfs torg 2,
T-Centralen T-bana, Ⓦ operan.se, charge.

The nineteenth-century Kungliga Operan is the proudest and most notable building on Gustav Adolfs Torg. King Gustav III, a great patron of the arts, founded the opera in 1773, and it was here that King Gustav III was shot at a masked ball in 1792 by one Captain Ankarström. The story is recorded in Verdi's opera *Un ballo in Maschera* (*The Masked Ball*), and you'll find Gustav's ball costume, as well as the assassin's pistols and mask, displayed in the Armoury in Gamla Stan. Swedes are proud of the Royal Opera's long and distinguished history; some of the world's greatest singers got their start here, from Jenny Lind, the nineteenth century 'Swedish Nightingale' who made a fabulously successful tour around the United States, to Jussi Bjorling and Birgit Nilsson. Though the opera's famous restaurant, Operakällaren which faces the water, is ruinously expensive, its trendy café, Bakfickan, is less so.

Medelhavsmuséet

MAP PAGE 36, POCKET MAP C11
Museum of Mediterranean and Near Eastern Antiquities. Fredsgatan 2, T-Centralen T-bana, Ⓦ varldskulturmuseerna.se/medelhavsmuseet, charge; free for under-19s.

Just off Gustav Adolfs Torg, and surrounded by several government ministries, the Medelhavsmuséet contains an excellent display on Egypt, including several whopping great mummies; the most attractive pieces, though, are the bronze weapons, tools and domestic objects from the time before the pharaohs. The Cyprus collections are also huge, the largest such assemblage outside the island itself, depicting the island civilization over a period of six thousand years. A couple of rooms examine Islamic culture through pottery, glass and metalwork, as well as decorative elements from architecture, Arabic calligraphy and Persian miniature painting.

Egypt display at Medelhavsmuseet

Shops

Beyond Retro

MAP PAGE 36, POCKET MAP C3
Drottninggatan 77, Rådmansgatan T-bana,
Ⓦ beyondretro.com.
There are two Beyond Retro
outlets in Stockholm; the one
on Drottninggatan is the biggest
vintage shop in Sweden, with over
14,000 items spread across its two
floors. Here you'll find floral dresses,
flannel shirts and more sequins than
you can shake a stick at! There's
even a pop-up Christmas jumper
shop if you're visiting in winter.

Designtorget

MAP PAGE 36, POCKET MAP B10
Sergels Torg 20, T-Centralen T-bana,
Ⓦ designtorget.se.
A shop for those looking for
something uniquely Swedish,
Designtorget is filled with trinkets
from Swedish designers – both
of the established and as-yet
undiscovered varieties. You'll find
all kinds of items here, from home
furnishings, kitchenware, artsy
postcards, books, toys and jewellery.
This outlet is their flagship store
and is the perfect spot to go gift-
hunting – either for someone else,
or, most likely, for yourself.

Gallerian

MAP PAGE 36, POCKET MAP C11
Hamngatan 37, T-Centralen T-bana,
Ⓦ gallerian.se.
Downtown Stockholm's first and
largest galleria is home to over 80
shops, cafés, bars and restaurants.
The shops here tend to be fairly
affordable, and are aimed at a
young, trendy crowd.

Hötorget flea market

MAP PAGE 36, POCKET MAP B10
Hötorget T-bana.
As well as the daily flower market,
Hötorget is also home to a flea
market that has taken place every
Sunday afternoon since the mid-
90s. It's choc-a-bloc with second-
hand books, records, kitchenware
and antiques, and is brilliant fun to
rummage through – whether you
find a treasure or not!

Illums Bolighus

MAP PAGE 36, POCKET MAP B11
Klarabergsgatan 62, T-Centralen T-bana,
Ⓦ illumsbolighus.com.
With a focus on Scandinavian design
and luxury goods, the building that
houses this Danish department
store was designed by one of the
most important modernist Swedish
architects, Sven Markelius. The staff
here are super friendly and helpful,
and you could easily spend a lot
of time getting lost amongst the
fascinating designs – even if you
don't end up buying anything.

NK

MAP PAGE 36, POCKET MAP C10
Hamngatan 18–20, Hötorget T-bana, Ⓦ nk.se.
NK (short for Nordiska Kompaniet
and pronounced a bit like 'encore')
is Sweden's biggest and most
luxurious department store.
Established in 1915, this is a store
steeped in history and tradition.
Under the rotating gold NK sign
you'll find men's and women's
fashion, make up and cosmetics,
ceramics and homeware, fine food
halls and much more – always with
a very chic Swedish focus on design.
Absolutely worth a visit, even just to
marvel at the building.

Cafés and food courts

Bakfickan

MAP PAGE 36, POCKET MAP C11
Gustav Adolfs Torg, Kungsträdgården
T-bana, Ⓦ operakallarensbakficka.se.
An intimate and charming counter
café-cum-restaurant with space for
just 28 guests, Bakfickan resembles
the snug of a British pub. It makes
for a sound choice for Swedish home
cooking (think cured salmon with
dill creamed potatoes), and is less

expensive and more laidback than the other dining option inside the Operhuset, Operakällaren. KrKrKr

Café Panorama

MAP PAGE 36, POCKET MAP C11
Sergels Torg 3, T-Centralen T-bana,
Ⓦ panoramacafe.se.

The top-floor café inside the Kulturhuset Stadsteatern has superb views over central Stockholm – make a beeline for one of the window tables. Lunch is dependable, always fresh and with several options usually including pasta, meat and a veggie choice. Lunch is very good value, especially taking into account the location – but it's also a great place for a coffee and cake stop. Kr

Hötorgshallen

MAP PAGE 36, POCKET MAP B10
Sergels Torg 29, Hötorget T-bana,
Ⓦ hotorgshallen.se.

Popular with Stockholm's office workers, this sprawling two-level food court is the place to come for fresh takeaway salads, wraps and kebabs. You'll find both prepared foods and ingredients here to suit all budgets – though the quality remains generally very good – so if you'd prefer a do-it-yourself option, you'll find everything you need here for a delicious picnic. KrKr

K25

MAP PAGE 36, POCKET MAP C10
Kungsgatan 25, Hötorget T-bana, Ⓦ k25.nu.
K25 is a bustling and modern food court stuffed to bursting with cheap and delicious food from all over the world, from dumplings and burgers to steaming bowls of Vietnamese pho; the Asian options here are particularly recommended. Grab a space to eat on one of the long tables amongst the office workers of Stockholm. Kr

Mellqvist Cafe & Bar

MAP PAGE 36, POCKET MAP B3
Rörstrandsgatan 4, St Eriksplan T-bana,
Ⓦ instagram.com/mellqvistkaffebar.
A busy café serving breakfast, lunch

and coffee that's popular with Swedish locals; it's bigger inside than it looks from the street, but it can still be hard to find a seat. It's well-loved for a reason, though – the dark roasted coffee is great and the cardamom buns here are particularly mouth-watering. This café was supposedly a favourite haunt of Stieg Larsson, and he is known to have penned much of the Millennium books series on his laptop here (see page 72). Kr

Vete-Katten

MAP PAGE 36, POCKET MAP B10
Kungsgatan 55, Hötorget T-bana,
Ⓦ vetekatten.se.

Delicious cakes and pastries fill the polished glass cabinets at this genteel, long-running coffee shop, which also does a good selection of cheap breakfasts and afternoon teas. The stars of its pastry menu are undoubtedly the princess cake and the vanilla bun, both of which are exceptional. Kr

Restaurants

Bistro Bestick

MAP PAGE 36, POCKET MAP B10
Bryggargatan 8, T-Centralen T-bana,
Ⓦ bistrobestick.se.

This restaurant is a sophisticated, compact, and contemporary Swedish bistro with stark white walls complemented by warm lighting and comfy sofas. It serves up tasty traditional home-cooking dishes (including the classic Swedish meatballs) with a focus on local ingredients. KrKr

Boqueria

MAP PAGE 36, POCKET MAP C10
Jakobsbergsgatan 17, Östermalmstorg T-bana, Ⓦ boqueriastockholm.se.
Boqueria is stylish, Spanish-themed tapas bar with a terrace based in the middle of a popular shopping mall called Mood. The food is here exceptional; the menu's main focus is, naturally, tapas, but there are

some tasty mains on offer too if you don't want to share. The Salmon Tartar Crispy Rice is particularly delectable, as is the deep-fried goat's cheese. A perfect stop for a brunch, lunch, dinner or just a drink. KrKr

Giro

MAP PAGE 36, POCKET MAP D3
Sveavägen 46, Östermalmstorg T-bana,
🌐 giropizzeria.se.

A vibrant a lively pizzeria, Giro is the result of a collaboration between the team behind the Nobis hotel (see page 108) and one of the world's oldest and most famous pizzerias, the Naples-based Da Michele. The Naples pizzeria makes only two pizzas, the margherita and the marinara – but the menu at Giro, offers many more options than just two; you'll find all your favourites here, as well as a few you'd never thought of – including some vegan options. What's more, all pizzas can be made gluten free. Kr

Operakällaren

MAP PAGE 36, POCKET MAP C11
Karl XII's Torg, T-Centralen T-bana,
🌐 operankallaren.se.

The Operahuset's famous restaurant and Sweden's most famous dining room has a magnificent setting with views across the water and over the Royal Palace. Dine on first-rate international delicacies in the lavish, oak-panelled room adorned with works of art. Very expensive, but definitely a smart choice for a really special evening. KrKrKrKr

Bars

The Auld Dub

MAP PAGE 36, POCKET MAP B10
Holländargatan 1, Hötorget T-bana,
🌐 theaulddub.se.

One of the busiest and most boisterous Irish pubs in town, with a traditional dark-wood interior and a large selection of foreign beers on tap and by the bottle. There's also live music most evenings.

Icebar

Berns

MAP PAGE 36, POCKET MAP D11
Berzelii Park, Nybroplan, Kungsträdgården
T-bana, 🌐 berns.se.

Originally made famous by writer August Strindberg, who picked up character ideas here for his novel, *The Red Room*, Berns is a unique, well-preserved 1860s art nouveau temple of entertainment and one of the chicest bars in town.

Fasching

MAP PAGE 36, POCKET MAP A10
Kungsgatan 63, Norrmalm, Hötorget
T-bana, 🌐 fasching.se.

If you're after local or foreign contemporary jazz, this is the place for you. Fasching is a long-established and legendary jazz club that also features an ambitious programme of salsa, soul and Latin. Can get quite crowded, which only adds to the atmosphere.

Icebar by Icehotel

MAP PAGE 36, POCKET MAP B11
Vasaplan 4, T-Centralen T-bana,
🌐 icebarstockholm.se.

The world's first permanent ice bar is made of ice from Swedish Lapland's famous Icehotel. A 45-minute visit includes a drink – the drink being the only thing in the whole place that isn't made of ice!

Kungsholmen

Just west of Norrmalm, Kungsholmen (King's Island) is a well-to-do area with wide, residential streets and large, leafy parks. It retains a quiet, neighbourhood feel and, at just under 4 sq km (1.5 sq miles), is very manageable to stroll around. The opening of the boutique shopping centre Vastermalmsgallerian, back in 2000, was the catalyst for a blossoming café, bistro and bar scene that's now thriving, and its numerous and attractive little restaurants offer an easy diversion from the bustle of the city.

Stockholms Stadshus

MAP PAGE 46, POCKET MAP A12
City Hall. Hantverkargatan 1, T-Centralen T-bana, Ⓦ stadshuset.stockholm, charge.
Finished in 1923, the majestic Stadsutset is one of the landmarks of modern Stockholm. When W.B. Yeats came to Stockholm in 1923 to receive the Nobel Prize for Literature, he took one look at the new City Hall and declared that "no work comparable in method and achievement has been accomplished since the Italian cities felt the excitement of the Renaissance," and honestly – it's hard not to agree with him.

Designed by Ragnar Östberg, the building rises gracefully and dramatically from the shore of Lake Mälaren. Artists and craftsmen from all over Sweden contributed to its creation, and it has become a fitting symbol almost an architectural hymn to the city. Stadshuset is worth several hours of your time, and even then you'll only get an inkling of what went into the construction of this remarkable building. The special hand-cut brick façades, made of over 8 million bricks; the imposing square tower capped by three golden crowns; the black granite reliefs, pillars and arches; all miraculously work together to form a unified and coherent whole, a monumental attempt to fuse the many different elements that make up Stockholm. It was inaugurated on Midsummer Day in 1923, the 400th anniversary of Gustav Vasa's coronation on the day he marched into town, and so has recently celebrated its hundredth birthday.

If you're a visiting head of state you'll be escorted from your boat up the elegant waterside steps; for lesser mortals, the only way to view the innards is on one of the guided tours, which reveal the Golden Hall, whose walls are covered with over 18 million glittering tiles arranged into intricate mosaics; stunning as the hall is, the artist was not overly experienced in making mosaics, so if you look towards the tops of the walls you might catch sight of a figure without a head where the artist ran out of room, a funny human detail that helps bring this other worldly room back down to earth. To the left of the Golden Hall is the huge glass-domed Blue Hall (which is actually red) where the Nobel Prize banquets are held, the prize that Alfred Nobel, the inventor of dynamite and over 350 other patents, established in his will (see page 47). There's also the Prince's Gallery, a long corridor with windows on one side and murals executed by Prince Eugen on the other. The murals are a reflection from the windows, the concept being that no matter where you're sitting in the room, you can enjoy always the view. The original idea was that all materials used in the construction and decoration were to be Swedish; however, the architect was faced with a problem when the French Government made a gift of the Tureholm tapestries, which were woven at Beauvais in France at the end of the seventeenth century. He resolved this by placing them in a rather small, round room. Today, this is where civil weddings are conducted; the happy couples have a choice of two ceremonies, one that lasts 3 minutes or one that lasts a miniscule 7 seconds. During Pride week in August, the City Hall plays host to colourful queer weddings en masse.

In a terraced garden by the water lie Carl Eldh's sculptures of the dramatist August Strindberg, the poet Gustaf Fröding and the painter Ernst Josephson. Also here, on top of a 14m (46ft) high column, is Christian Eriksson's bronze statue of Engelbrekt, Sweden's great hero of the Middle Ages.

In summer, don't miss climbing to the top of the 115m (350ft) tall City Hall Tower for a superb view of the Old Town, central Stockholm and Lake Mälaren.

Index – The Swedish Contemporary Art Foundation

MAP PAGE 46, POCKET MAP A11
Kungsbro strand 19, T-Centralen T-bana,
Ⓦ indexfoundation.se, free.

Small but sweet, Index has been active since 1974 and is a diverting way to spend a contemplative hour. It started out as a magazine focusing on Scandinavian photography and contemporary art; then, in 2011 it opened its current exhibition hall. These days, Index is a gallery where artists are invited to showcase their work, conduct research and interact with their audience through events and readings – if you're lucky, you might catch a show or a poetry reading which tend to be interesting and entertaining. The programme of exhibitions and events is eclectic, and could cover anything from zines to photography to sculpture to film, so it's worth checking out. The staff are knowledgeable and friendly, and happy to answer questions about the works on show.

The Blue Hall at the Stadshus

Kronobergsparken

MAP PAGE 46, POCKET MAP A4–B4

Fridhemsplan T-Bana.

West of City Hall and located close to the centre of Kungsholmen, Kronobergsparken is a nice spot for a stroll, with plenty of benches to stop for a picnic. Formerly the site of a mill, it was made into a public park in the early years of the twentieth century and is now a quiet oasis beloved by Kungsholmen's residents. There's an adult workout area, a basketball court, two dog parks and two children's playgrounds amidst the greenery and hills – perfect for sledging if it happens to snow on your visit.

Norr Mälarstrand

MAP PAGE 46, POCKET MAP A5–C5

Rådhuset T-bana.

Extending west of Stadshuset is Norr Mälarstrand, a pretty tree-lined promenade that follows the water's edge all the way to the Västerbron bridge. This pleasant walk has lovely views out across Lake Mälaren and across to Södermalm on the other side, and is often crowded with Stockholmers out for a casual stroll or a jog. It's especially popular on a sunny Sunday afternoon, but it's equally as beautiful in the colder months too; just be sure to wrap up and treat yourself to a coffee to keep you warm on the walk. This is also a lovely spot to watch the sun set, and while the Northern Lights only make rare appearances in Stockholm, this is the best place to catch them if they are forecast.

Rålambshåvsparken

MAP PAGE 46, POCKET MAP A5

Fridhemsplan T-Bana.

At the western end of Norr Mälarstrand is one of Stockholm's most beloved and popular parks. Rålambshåvsparken, also called Rålis, is located between two

The pacifist who invented dynamite

Alfred Nobel (1833–96) became a first-rate chemist while still in his teens. Inventor, engineer and industrialist, he held a total of 355 patents during his lifetime. A pacifist at heart, he invented dynamite, which proved a boon to modern warfare. Nobel also patented blasting gelatin, and invented smokeless gunpowder. These products formed the basis of his industrial empire, which spread across five continents. Alfred Nobel established the celebrated Nobel prizes in his will, drawn up a year before his death. These were for physics and chemistry (awarded by the Swedish Academy of Sciences), for physiological or medical works (awarded by the Karolinska Institute in Stockholm), for literature (awarded by the Academy in Stockholm), and for champions of peace (awarded by a committee of five elected by the Norwegian Storting). They were to go to those who 'shall have conferred the greatest benefit on mankind' with the stipulation that 'no consideration whatever shall be given to the nationality of the candidates'. His entire fortune was dedicated to this purpose. First awarded in 1901, the prizes for the first four categories have been given at the Nobel Dinner held at Stockholm's Stadshuset (City Hall) on 10 December each year. Nobel directed that the Peace prize be awarded in Oslo, which at his death, and until 1905, was part of Sweden.

Kungsholmen

CAFÉS	
By:fiket	1
Café Frankfurt	3
Café Portiken	6
Komet Café	4

RESTAURANTS	
AG	2
The Green Queen	8
Mälarpaviljongen	9
Mäster Anders	5
Stadshuskällaren	7

BARS	
Boulebar Rålambshov	1
Chewie's	2
Orangeriet	3

SHOPS	
59 Vintage	4
Hugo	2
MiNilla	1
Ting från förr och nu	3

ACCOMMODATION	
Clarion Hotel Amaranten	4
Connect City	2
M/S Monika	1
Stockholm Hostel	3

Index – The Swedish Contemporary Art Foundation

popular residential areas, with a great view over Riddarfjärden, City Hall, and Gamla Stan. This park is a hive of physical activity, and you're likely to see people playing football, basketball, volleyball, boule and softball amongst the joggers, skaters, windsurfers and outdoor swimmers that flock here in all weathers. Outdoor exercise and yoga classes often take place here in the summer, and there's also an amphitheatre and several kids' playgrounds.

Smedsuddsbadet

MAP PAGE 46, POCKET MAP A4
Fridhemsplan T–Bana, free.

Just south of Rålambshåvsparken is an excellent sandy beach, Smedsuddsbadet, which enjoys fantastic views of the Stadhuset and the Old Town. This place is free, and super popular amongst families and swimmers, with a diving board into the lake as well as showers and toilets. There's a wooden walkway down into the water making it accessible for wheelchair users and a large grassy area for those who'd like to catch some rays, while a lovely little café supplies beachgoers with hotdogs

Smedsuddsbadet

and ice cream. You can find kayaks and stand-up paddleboards on the eastern side, and there's also a wooden walkway running along the beach that's a gorgeous place to go for a run. The beach is usually fairly quiet in the mornings, but can get more crowded towards lunchtime and into the afternoon, especially on hot days; in the evening it turns into something of a party hotspot, when the tranquillity of the morning is entirely forgotten.

Fredhällsbadet

MAP PAGE 46, POCKET MAP A4
Kristineberg T-bana, free.

One for experienced swimmers because of its easy access to deep water, Fredhällsbadet is gorgeous in the summer when Stockholm enjoys long hours of daylight. There are no shallows here; you can access the water from steps and jetties from the cliffs, though the braver souls jump directly from the rocks into Lake Mälaren to cool off. On warm days, you'll find a sunbather on every available rock or patch of grass soaking up the rays or having a picnic. Fredhällsbadet tends to close early, but the nearby cliffs of Fredhällsklipporna make also make gorgeous unofficial swimming spots, and are also lovely places to catch the sunset on a summer's evening.

Hornsbergs Strandpark

MAP PAGE 46, POCKET MAP A3

Located on the northern shore of Kungsholmen, Hornsbergs Strandpark is another park that's lovely for swimming and bathing during the summer months. The park was finished in 2012, when it received an architectural award. There's a path running along the water that has several great spots for a nice summer swim along the way. Perhaps one of the most relaxed parks on Kungsholmen, you'll often find people barbecuing here, and even live music around the park on warm days. It's especially beautiful at sunset.

Shops

59 Vintage

MAP PAGE 46, POCKET MAP B5
Hantverkargatan 59, Rådhuset T-bana,
ⓦ 59vintagestore.se.

A genuine vintage shop with branded vintage items, 59 Vintage is a real treasure trove. The shop is well organised and it's usually easy to find what you're looking for, but if you need any help or have questions, the owner is extremely kind and helpful. Particularly good for women's clothes; it can be a little light on the menswear side of things.

Hugo

MAP PAGE 46, POCKET MAP A4
Sankt Eriksgatan 39, Fridhemsplan T-bana,
ⓦ hugo-sthlm.com.

A stylish menswear boutique, Hugo has been based at the same location since it opened in 1978. The aim is to carefully curate a collection of fashion brands that create timeless pieces without breaking the bank. This is a small business with super attentive and friendly staff who will help you out, and as such has become a real trusted name in Stockholm – its customers swear by it. You can buy pretty much anything here and even though the brands are international, you can be quite sure that you're rocking the Scandi chic.

MiNilla

MAP PAGE 46, POCKET MAP B4
Fleminggatan 69, Fridhemsplan T-bana,
ⓦ minilla.se.

A really fun little shop that's great for gift shopping – for someone else, or for yourself. There's a good selection of colourful women's clothes, accessories, scarves, jewellery and bags, as well as furnishings and funny little oddities like jewelled candles and gemstones.

Ting från förr och nu

MAP PAGE 46, POCKET MAP A4
Hantverkargatan 81, Fridhemsplan T-bana,
ⓦ instagram.com/tingfranforrochnu.

Ting från förr och nu means 'things from the past and present', which is exactly what you'll find at this gorgeous retro boutique. There's a huge range of affordable vintage treasures here, and some genuine bargains. The owner, Linda, is super stylish and very helpful – her Instagram page is full of pictures of her own personal style and items you can find in the shop. She even has a Youtube channel!

Cafés

By:fiket

MAP PAGE 46, POCKET MAP A3
Franzéngatan 1A, Stadshagen T-bana,
ⓦ instagram.com/byfiket.

A relaxed, quiet café with a focus on local – often organic – produce and simple (but very well done and beautifully presented) food that stems from the Federation of Swedish Farmers. The daily hot specials are posted weekly on their Instagram page, and tend to feature classic Swedish fixtures such as wallenbergare (breadcrumbed veal) and raggmunk (a potato pancake), but also more contemporary favourites such as Teriyaki chicken or pulled pork. All pastries are made on-site, and are best enjoyed on the shores of the nearby Karlbergssjön canal. Kr

Café Frankfurt

MAP PAGE 46, POCKET MAP B4
Pipersgatan 24, Rådhuset T-bana,
ⓦ cafefrankfurt.se.

A small café close to the City Hall, Café Frankfurt's specialty is its crispy, chewy, Montréal-style bagels served with your choice of filling: smoked salmon, strawberry jam or their own house-made cream cheese. They've recently been experimenting with sourdough bagels, and also do very good coffee. Kr

Mälarpaviljongen

Café Portiken

MAP PAGE 46, POCKET MAP A12
Hantverkargatan 2A, Rådhuset T-bana.
An unassuming, old-school, no-frills Swedish café, run by really lovely jolly ladies. Located in the gatehouse of Serafim Park, Café Portiken serves sandwiches, fika, and lunch every weekday; they do especially good soups and coffee. Super affordable (cheap, even!), and popular with Stockholm's more senior citizens – but very welcoming to those of a more junior disposition. Kr

Komet Café

MAP PAGE 46, POCKET MAP A11
Kungsholmsgatan 10, Rådhuset T-bana,
Ⓦ kometstockholm.wordpress.com.
Komet opened its doors in 2021 and has already become one of the most popular cafés on Kungsholmen. Its interior is minimalist white with trendy black cups and plates. They serve French classics, like pains au chocolat and enormous croissants which are often cited as the best in Stockholm, as well as Swedish favourites like cinnamon buns and seasonal semlas. The coffee here is top notch and the lunchtime sandwiches are brilliant (and many are vegetarian). Kr

Restaurants

AG

MAP PAGE 46, POCKET MAP B4
Kronobergsgatan 37, Fridhemsplan T-bana,
Ⓦ restaurangag.se.
There are some incredible vegan restaurants in Stockholm, but AG is not one of them; the self-declared best meat restaurant in Stockholm is decidedly one for the carnivores. Set in an old silver factory (the eagle-eyed reader will have noticed that AG is the chemical symbol for silver), AG immediately became the most happening place to have dinner when it opened in 2011, despite its somewhat out-of-the-way location. The steaks are tenderized onsite in a large fridge that can be inspected as you take your seats, and they also have an incredible wine list – it's 115 pages long. KrKrKrKr

The Green Queen

MAP PAGE 46, POCKET MAP B5
Norr Mälarstrand 64, Fridhemsplan T-bana,
Ⓦ thegreenqueensthlm.com.
It feels like a flower shop when you walk inside, but the Green Queen is actually a plant-based restaurant – one that the even the carnivores won't want to miss. This little restaurant serves up all the staples of a fast-food joint including burgers, quesadillas, and kebabs, and snacks – but plant-based, and they really get it right. The restaurant is located on the gorgeous Norr Mälarstrand, which makes it an ideal take away-spot if you want to have lunch at the pontoons just across the street or just around the corner in the Rålambshovs Park. Kr

Mälarpaviljongen

MAP PAGE 46, POCKET MAP B5
Norr Mälarstrand 64, Fridhemsplan T-bana,
Ⓦ ny.malarpaviljongen.se.

This stunningly verdant waterside oasis is absolutely not to be missed. It's an LGBTQ+-owned, summer-only restaurant, café and bar on a floating pontoon strung with colourful fairylights and blooming flowers with a stunning view of the waters of Riddarfjärden. The restaurant is incredibly atmospheric and serves creative, seasonal menus with great plant-based options. Their house rosé is to die for, and a portion of the price of every glass or bottle goes to the Rainbow Foundation, a charity that works to protect queer people from countries where they are persecuted and discriminated against. After finishing your food, head to the high-spirited bar with that plays brilliant music. KrKr

Mäster Anders

MAP PAGE 46, POCKET MAP B5
Pipersgatan 1, Rådhuset T-bana,
Ⓦ masteranders.se.
A very pleasant eatery that dates from 1905, and which has preserved the turn-of-the-century style in features including the beautiful tiled floor and mirrors on the walls. The menu is Swedish and French-inspired and dominated by beautifully prepared meat dishes, with an open-to-view kitchen. Excellent service and a good wine list. KrKrKr

Stadshuskällaren

MAP PAGE 46, POCKET MAP A12
Stadshuset, T-Centralen T-bana,
Ⓦ stadshuskallarensthlm.se.
Found in the basement of City Hall, the restaurant serves contemporary Swedish cuisine under beautiful arched ceilings. In fact, it's here that you'll have the chance to savour the same dishes and wines served to the Nobel Prize winners the previous December – even if you haven't had a chance to knock 'win a Nobel Prize' off your to do list just yet. Excellent personal service, as you might expect. KrKrKr

Bars

Boulebar Rålambshov

MAP PAGE 46, POCKET MAP A5
Multiple locations, Ⓦ boulebar.se.
Swedes love a game of boule to go with their beer on a warm summer's evening. There are five Boulebar locations in Stockholm, two of which are on Kungsholmen – Rålambshov and Rådhuset, both of which have magical waterside locations. The restaurant serves classic French dishes for lunch, dinner, and brunch at weekends – a perfect pitstop while you wait for a pitch to become free.

Chewie's

MAP PAGE 46, POCKET MAP B5
Norr Mälarstrand 32, Rådhuset T-bana,
Ⓦ chewiesbar.com.
This must be the friendliest wine bar in the world, with helpful and non-pretentious advice on hand for those who are overwhelmed by the extensive list of natural wines and craft beer. The owners, Ali and Viktor, make much of the all-vegan menu onsite, including vegan cheese that is actually good! There are board games scattered around and the bar's namesake, a very good dog called Chewie, greets you enthusiastically at the door.

Orangeriet

MAP PAGE 46, POCKET MAP B5
Norr Mälarstrand Kajplats 46, Rådhuset T-bana, Ⓦ trattorian.se/orangeriet.
This lively cocktail bar and outdoor restaurant is located on the Norr Mälarstrand waterfront. Serving very good pizzas and even better cocktails, the bartenders here are outstanding. The stylish decor is reminiscent of English gardens with more than a hint of the country chic about it. Overall, a welcoming and upbeat family- and dog-friendly choice with good vegan options, and live DJs later on in the evening.

Djurgården

It's easy to see why Stockholmers love Djurgården, Stockholm's most enjoyable city park. Pronounced 'Yoor-gorden', this immense, largely unspoiled island of natural beauty offers the perfect escape from hectic city life; it was used as a royal hunting park between the sixteenth and eighteenth centuries, and is still controlled by the king to this day. In addition to miles of woodland trails and magnificent oaks, some of which go back to Viking times, it contains outdoor coffee shops and restaurants tucked away amidst its greenery, as well as an amusement park and some of the city's principal museums. Djurgården is perfect for picnicking, jogging, horse riding, or just enjoying a quiet walk; but if you're heading to the museums, be sure to leave a full day or two to fit everything in – you'll need it!

Nordiska Museet

MAP PAGE 54, POCKET MAP F5
Nordic Museum. Djurgårdsvägen 6,
Ⓦ nordiskamuseet.se, charge.

The palatial Nordiska Museet, just over Djurgårdsbron from Strandvägen, provides a good grounding in what has made the Swedish nation tick from the sixteenth century to the present. The displays of trends and traditions are a valiant attempt to represent the last five hundred years of Swedish cultural history and folk art in an accessible fashion, with household furniture, items of clothing and other bits and bobs for perusal. On the ground floor of the cathedral-like interior, you can't fail to spot Carl Milles's phenomenal oak statue of Gustav Vasa (1496–1560), the sixteenth-century king who drove out the Danes and the father of modern Sweden; but there are more than 1 million objects to view here. You'll find exhibits depicting the history of upper-class fashions, an interesting section on food and drink with table settings from different periods, and a costume gallery devoted to Swedish peasant dress from the beginning of the ninth century. There's also a feature on the nomadic Lapps and their reindeer and an exhibition concentrating on Nordic folk art that includes Swedish wall paintings, Norwegian tapestries, Finnish drinking vessels and Danish embroidery.

Vasamuseet

MAP PAGE 54, POCKET MAP F5
Vasa Museum. Galärvarvsvägen 14,
Ⓦ vasamuseet.se, charge; free for under-18s.

Housed in an oddly shaped building close to the Nordiska Museet, the Vasamuseet is Stockholm's most popular museum and stands head and shoulders above Stockholm's other museums. In many ways, you could say that this museum is a monument to what was, in its day, a complete failure. It contains the world's best-preserved seventeenth-century warship, the Vasa, which was built on the orders of King Gustav II Adolf, but sank in Stockholm harbour on her maiden voyage in

1628 – just fifteen minutes after setting sail. A victim of engineering miscalculation, the Vasa's hull was too narrow to withstand even the slightest swell which, when coupled with top-heavy rigging, made her a maritime disaster waiting to happen. On the 10th of August, she went down barely a few hundred metres from her moorings. Preserved in mud at the bottom of the harbour for three hundred and thirty-three years, the ship was raised along with twelve thousand objects in 1961, and now forms the centrepiece of the museum. Raising her from the deep took years of planning; there were several interesting methods of retrieval suggested, including encasing her in a giant ice cube and floating her to the surface. Another idea was to fill her with ping pong balls, but unfortunately, not enough balls could be sourced, so the idea was scrapped in favour of a more sensible method involving tunnels, ropes and floating pontoons. Her retrieval was a huge event; it was the first event ever to be broadcast live on Swedish TV, and members of the public who didn't own a television set crowded round screens in shop windows in order to watch her masts break the water. Impressive though the building is, nothing prepares you for the sheer size of the ship: 226ft (69m) long, the main mast originally 164ft (50m) above the keel, it sits virtually complete in a cradle of supporting mechanical tackle. Surrounding walkways bring you nose-to-nose with cannon hatches and restored decorative relief, the gilded wooden sculptures on the soaring prow designed to intimidate the enemy and proclaim Swedish might. Carved into the ship's stern, the resplendent figures of two naked cherubs with podgy stomachs and rosy cheeks, proudly bearing the Swedish crown between them, are truly remarkable for their fine detail and garish colours.

Adjacent exhibition halls and presentations on several levels take care of all the retrieved items, which give an invaluable insight into life on board – you can find preserved pottery, coins, pewter tankards, glassware, clay pipes, cannonballs and items of clothing taken from the skeletons of

Vasamuseet

eighteen seamen found on the ship. Among the oddest discoveries were a box containing butter – rancid, of course – and a flask of rum, still drinkable after more than three centuries. There are reconstructions of life on board, detailed models of the Vasa, displays relating to contemporary social and political life and a fascinating film of the rescue operation. Children will especially enjoy 'sailing' the Vasa using computer simulators.

Spiritmuseum

MAP PAGE 54, POCKET MAP F5
Spirit Museum. Djurgårdsstrand 9,
ⓦ spritmuseum.se, charge.
From the Vasamuseet it's only a hop to the Spritmuseum, a unique museum all about the Swedes' bittersweet relationship with alcohol. An odd little place filled with any- and everything to do with booze – from the science of distilling vodka and

brewing beer to alcohol-inspired art. It's fairly interactive, with lots of opportunities to taste and smell ingredients as well as get involved in amusing quizzes – but it's also a great opportunity to learn more about the Swedes' attitude to alcohol and the culture surrounding drinking. A visit to the museum bar afterwards is, of course, a must.

Viking Museum

MAP PAGE 54, POCKET MAP F5
Djurgårdsvägen 48,
ⓦ thevikingmuseum.com, charge.
The Viking Museum is relatively small, but still manages to provide a fascinating look at Viking life as it really was – be prepared for some of the classic images you might have to be challenged! Find out how Vikings lived, what they ate, and exactly how much truth there is in their fearsome seafaring reputation in an interactive, almost immersive

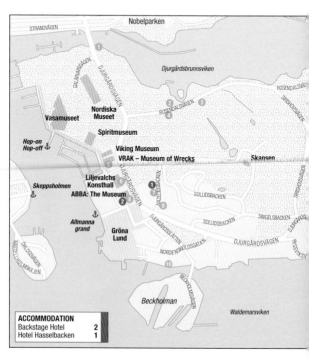

ACCOMMODATION
Backstage Hotel 2
Hotel Hasselbacken 1

way – the staff are dressed in Viking attire and have fantastic storytelling skills, as well as being incredibly friendly and knowledgeable. The museum ends with a delightful surprise – a historical ride that lasts around 10 minutes and takes you through a Viking story to round off your visit.

VRAK – Museum of Wrecks

MAP PAGE 54, POCKET MAP F5
Djurgårdsstrand 17, Ⓦ vrak.se, charge.
Next door to the Viking Museum, you'll find the newest addition to the island's attractions: VRAK. Opened in late 2021, Vrak is a small but thoughtful maritime archaeology museum; reflective of the distinctive location it occupies, nowhere else in the world are there as many well-preserved wooden wrecks as there are in the Baltic Sea. There are a number of reasons for this: the fact that the water

is very cold, dark, oxygen-poor and brackish all act as brilliant preservatives for wood and textiles. These conditions also mean that shipworms – so-called because they are notorious for boring holes into and eventually destroying wood that is immersed in the sea – can't survive in these waters, meaning that many wooden ships that sink remain almost entirely intact. With the help of digital technology and interactive exhibits, Vrak takes visitors on a deep dive to the bottom of the ocean, whilst leaving the shipwrecks undisturbed on the ocean floor where they are best preserved. It will be a quieter and more relaxed place to learn about shipwrecks than the Vasa Museum, which gets crowded.

Liljevalchs Konsthall

MAP PAGE 54, POCKET MAP F5
Djurgårdsvägen 60, Ⓦ liljevalchs.se, charge; free for under-18s and on Mondays.

Djurgården

CAFÉS	
Blå Porten	1
Flickorna Helin	3
Konsthallen	6
Mackverket Vrak Café & Bar	5
Skroten	10

RESTAURANTS	
AIRA	11
Cirkus Restaurang	9
Hasselbacken	7
Pop Story	8
Ulla Winbladh	4
Villa Godthem	2

Rosendals Slott

Djurgården

Prins Eugens Waldemarsudde

Biskopsuddens Marina

Thielska Galleriet

N

| 0 | metres | 200 |
| 0 | yards | 200 |

Liljevalchs Konsthall is a gorgeous exhibition space; the redbrick building that dates from 1916 and was the first independent and public art gallery for contemporary art in Sweden. It has recently been joined by a sleek white companion, added in 2021. It mounts excellent exhibitions of paintings, sculpture and handicrafts, often with a focus on modern local artists, and is inclusive in its values; it aims to be interesting to generalists and newcomers to the modern art world, as well as to those with very specific artistic interests. A recurring feature is the ever-popular Vårsalongen (Spring Salon) which has run between January to March almost every year since 1921; the Salon is open for anyone over the age of 18 to apply to, and the resulting artworks are judged by a jury.

of Sweden's most famous band; even those with only a passing interest will find something here to make them smile. Highlights include outfits worn by the fab four, as well as a reconstruction of Polar Studios, where three of the band's last albums were recorded. There's even a piano that, it's said, is hooked up to Benny Andersson's own. If, and when, he twinkles the ivories, you'll hear the tunes he's playing. There's also a red phone in the museum, and if it rings, you'd better be sure to answer it – a member of the band will be on the other line! It's creatively designed, very interactive and a whole lot of fun; if you've ever fancied getting up on stage as the fifth member of ABBA, singing karaoke at Polar Studios and or dancing in an ABBA music video – now's your chance!

ABBA: The Museum

MAP PAGE 54, POCKET MAP F5
Djurgårdsvägen 68,
Ⓦ abbathemuseum.com, charge.

The all-singing, all-dancing ABBA museum is a must for lifelong fans

Gröna Lund

MAP PAGE 54, POCKET MAP F6
Lilla Allmänna Gränd 9, Ⓦ gronalund.com, charge.

Gröna Lund, or Tivoli, is Stockholm's tasteful amusement

Sweden's fab four

Overturning odds of 20–1, Anni-Frid Lyngstad, Benny Andersson, Björn Ulvæus and Agnetha Fältskog first came to the world's attention as they stormed to victory in April 1974 at the Eurovision Song Contest – tellingly, the first year in which the public were able to vote – with their now famous ditty, *Waterloo*. ABBA went on to become the biggest-selling group in the world, topping the charts for a decade with hits like *Dancing Queen* (performed to celebrate the marriage of Swedish King Carl Gustaf to German commoner Silvia Sommerlath in 1976), *Mamma Mia* and *Money Money Money*. However, the relentless workload of recording and touring took its toll; frictions within the group surfaced, the two couples – Agnetha and Björn, and Anni-Frid and Benny – divorced, and ABBA called it a day in 1983. Having mostly withdrawn from public life, Agnetha now lives a quiet life on the island of Ekerö on Lake Mälaren. Anni-Frid married a German prince, lives in Switzerland and spends her time championing environmental causes. Björn is back in Stockholm where he partly owns the domestic airline, Nextjet, and writes and produces music with Benny, who has opened his own hotel on Södermalm, Rival (see page 111).

park. In addition to its spectacular setting, it contains over thirty rides and rollercoasters, numerous restaurants, fast food outlets and bars, a first-rate theatre, and an open-air stage where top Swedish and foreign entertainers perform. The talk of the park is still the ominous Fritt Fall Tilt, which involves being catapulted face-first towards the ground from on high – this is definitely one for before lunch. It's not open all year round, so be sure to check online before you make plans.

Skansen

MAP PAGE 54, POCKET MAP G5
Djurgårdsslätten 49–51, ⓦ skansen.se, charge.

It's Skansen that most people come to Djurgården for: the world's first open air museum is vast, with 150 buildings, both reconstructed and real, from before the industrial era laid out on a region-by-region basis. Created by Artur Hazelius in 1891, the idea behind Skansen was to establish a kind of miniature Sweden, showing how Swedish people, from farmers to aristocrats, lived and worked during different eras. Gathered here are reassembled cottages, manor houses, peasant and Lapp huts, and ancient farmsteads that have been transported from all over Sweden; they are complete with cows, pigs and other farm animals, not to mention the staff who wander around in costume to recreate the atmosphere of what life was really like in Sweden at the time. Country stores and city shops – including an old pharmacy and a bakery that makes very good cinnamon buns – and the eighteenth-century Seglora Kyrka, popular for weddings, dot the area. Glassblowers, potters, bookbinders and goldsmiths are among the craftsmen plying their trade in the workshops. You can also potter around a zoo (containing Nordic animals such as brown bears, elk and reindeer,

Gröna Lund

as well as non-native species like monkeys), and an aquarium with poisonous snakes and turtles.

Partly because of the attention paid to accuracy, and partly due to the admirable lack of commercialization, Skansen manages to avoid tackiness: even the snack bars dole out traditional foods and in winter serve up great bowls of warming soup. Skansen is an absolute delight for all ages; there is always something going on and you can easily spend a whole day or more here without any risk of getting bored. The park is also a pleasant spot to visit on summer evenings when there are special programmes, including live music concerts on Tuesdays, and the view from the hilltop of the lights of Stockholm glittering in all directions off the surrounding waters is spectacular.

Prins Eugens Waldemarsudde

MAP PAGE 54, POCKET MAP H6
Prins Eugens Väg 6, ⓦ waldemarsudde.se, charge.

"Second to the arts, I think flowers are my greatest joy," wrote Prince

Thielska Galleriet

Eugen in 1901. Widely known as
Sweden's 'Painter Prince' and one of
the most accomplished landscape
painters of his generation, this is
Prince Eugen's former house and
art gallery – and it is his two great
loves, art and flowers, that make
this place such a pleasure to visit.
When he died in 1947 at the age
of 82, he bequeathed his property
to the nation. The public can visit
the house – where the ground
floor offers a fascinating insight
into his lifestyle – and the gallery,
in a lovely setting of parkland and
terraced flower gardens that slope
down to a channel of the Baltic Sea.
Waldemarsudde has an ambitious
collection of Swedish paintings,
mostly from the late nineteenth
and early twentieth centuries. There
are also more than a hundred works
by the prince himself, and the
garden contains a number of really
gorgeous sculptures.

Rosendals Slott

MAP PAGE 54, POCKET MAP H5
Rosendal Palace. Rosendalsvägen 49,
Ⓦ kungligaslotten.se, charge.
Also on the southern bank of the
island is the summer retreat of

King Karl XIV Johan. Built in
the 1820s, Rosendals Slott was
one of Sweden's first prefabricated
homes. In 1913 it was opened to
the public as a museum devoted to
the life and times of the king, and
it remains a highly impressive work
of historic restoration. The decor
is magnificent, with Swedish-made
furniture and richly woven textiles
in brilliant colours. It is not open
all year round, so be sure to check
online before you make the trip.

Thielska Galleriet

MAP PAGE 54, POCKET MAP H6
Thiel Gallery. Sjötullsbacken 6–8,
Ⓦ thielska-galleriet.se, charge; under-19s
free.
At the far eastern end of
Djurgården, known as
Blockhusudden, the Thielska
Galleriet is one of Stockholm's
major treasures, a fine example
of both Swedish architecture
and Nordic art. The house was
built by Ferdinand Boberg (who
also designed Prince Eugens
Waldermarsudde and the NK
department store, see page 41)
at the turn of the twentieth
century for banker and art
connoisseur Ernest Thiel, and
turned into an art gallery after he
sold it to the state in 1924. Thiel
knew many contemporary Nordic
artists personally and gathered an
impressive collection of paintings
over the years, many of which are
on show today. There are works by
Carl Larsson, Anders Zorn – most
notably his portraits and female
nudes – Edvard Munch, Bruno
Liljefors and August Strindberg,
whose paintings of wild Swedish
landscapes are displayed. Guided
tours are available to book online
and last for around an hour. The
museum enjoys a dramatic setting
at the very tip of Djurgården;
indeed, the views out over
Stockholm harbour and across
to the district of Nacka on the
southern shore alone warrant a
trip out here.

Cafés

Blå Porten

MAP PAGE 54, POCKET MAP F4

Djurgårdsvägen 64, Ⓦ blaporten.com.
Blå is a classic destination for
Stockholmers on a weekend
walk or a visit to the museums
of Djurgården. This glorious café
is set in a stunning glass-walled
building overlooking a bohemian
courtyard with outdoor seating
around an old fountain. The open
sandwiches and lunches here are
Provençal-influenced and include a
wide choice of quiches, pies, salads
and soups, including vegetarian
options. There are also tempting
pastries on offer for those with a
sweet tooth! Kr

Flickorna Helin

MAP PAGE 54, POCKET MAP G5

Rosendalsvägen 14, Ⓦ flickornahelin.se.
This charming self-serve café has
a very relaxed atmosphere. The
castle-like building is located along
the pedestrian path on Djurgården,
and it's a splendid place for lunch
or a caffeine break to refuel
between visits to the island's various
museums; choose from their
particularly popular selection of
delectable baked goods and find a
seat on the terrace overlooking the
garden. They also do flavoursome
and healthy salads and sandwiches.
Both salads and cakes come in
pleasingly large portions. Kr

Konsthallen

MAP PAGE 54, POCKET MAP F5

Allmänna gränd 2, Ⓦ konsthallen.com.
Konsthallen is a seafood café and
bakery with more than a touch of
the Wes Anderson about it – think
tiled floors and kitsch mint-green
fittings. Serves very good lunches
such as toasties, as well as great
pastries if you're looking for
something a little less substantial.
Surprisingly calm and cosy
considering the location – it's right
next to the ABBA Museum, so it

makes for a perfect stop to refuel
after all that singing. Kr

Mackverket Vrak Café & Bar

MAP PAGE 54, POCKET MAP F5

Djurgårdsstrand 17, Ⓦ vrak.se.
Located inside VRAK (see page
55), Mackverket serves hearty
sourdough sandwiches with
seasonal fillings of fresh veg and
meat from Swedish producers. The
restaurant started life as a food
truck, which still exists – but now
they also operate three permanent
restaurants. Kids options are
available, as well as coffee, sweets,
and some beers. Service is fast and
friendly, making it the perfect place
for a pitstop before continuing
your museum escapade. Kr

Skroten

MAP PAGE 54, POCKET MAP G6

Beckholmsvägen 14, Ⓦ skrotens.se.
Having started life at the old
marine store on Skeppsholmen,
Skroten is now located at the
shipyard on Djurgården, slightly
hidden away in a side street. It's
a totally charming place, with
wooden floors and fairy lights

Flickorna Helin

galore, as well as lovely outdoor seating for when the weather holds up and a delicious menu; the fish stew is particularly good. Stop for a coffee or stay for a lunch and a glass of wine. Kr

Restaurants

AIRA
MAP PAGE 54, POCKET MAP H6
Biskopsvägen 9, Ⓦ aira.se.
After opening in 2020, fine-dining restaurant AIRA received its second Michelin star in 2023. Set in a stunning glass-fronted building that allows the interior to be full of natural light, the kitchen focuses on seasonal Nordic ingredients and traditional cooking. You can opt for the set menu or splash out on the tasting menu for a few bites of everything – think wood smoked arctic char, wood-fire grilled quail and caviar. Stunning in every way, but with prices to match – one for a special occasion! KrKrKrKr

Cirkus Restaurang
MAP PAGE 54, POCKET MAP G5
Djurgårdsslätten 43-45, Ⓦ cirkus.se.
Cirkus is a historic events venue that opened in 1892, originally – as

Cirkus

the name suggests – as a circus; in fact, it still has a lift suitable for transporting elephants, should the need ever arise. Since then, it has come to play host to all manner of concerts, plays, shows and spectacles. Their restaurant is a creative and playful bistro inspired by the venue's colourful history, and is set in an absolutely gorgeous, high-ceilinged, glass room reminiscent of a greenhouse but without the stifling temperatures. The menu focuses mainly on dishes with French, Asian and American influences, and they have a surprisingly reasonably priced chef's table. A fabulous place for a coffee, cocktail, or dinner. KrKrKr

Hasselbacken
MAP PAGE 54, POCKET MAP G5
Hazeliusbacken 20, Ⓦ hasselbacken.com.
The restaurant at Hotel Hasselbacken serves delicious breakfast, lunch, dinner and drinks in a historical setting that dates back to 1748. This is the place to come for classic Swedish dishes with a modern touch. The menu changes weekly, but Hasselback potatoes are, of course, a permanent feature, since the dish was created here in 1953 by one of the restaurant's trainee chefs;

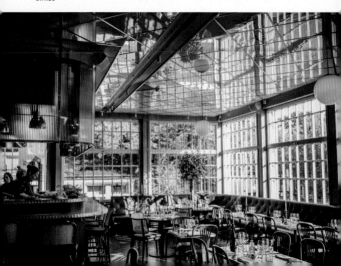

Hasselbacken

they come with toppings including salmon, dill cream and horseradish, goat's cheese, pine nuts and rosemary, and seaweed caviar, sour cream and red onions – but by far and away the most delicious are the truffle mayonnaise and parmesan. If the weather holds out, you can eat outside on the sun-filled on the terrace. KrKr

Pop Story

MAP PAGE 54, POCKET MAP F5
Djurgårdsvägen 68, Ⓦ popstory.se.
All bright, blocky colours and pop art, Popstory is a vibrant assault on the senses in the best way. They do a good brunch menu featuring all the classic favourites, and a lunch menu mostly revolving around upscale burgers and fries. They often have DJs and live bands, and if you fancy making music of your own, there's a karaoke booth where you can sing Norwegian karaoke – the singer wears headphones and sings along to their chosen tune, while everyone else has to guess the song from their singing alone! KrKrKr

Ulla Winbladh

MAP PAGE 54, POCKET MAP G5
Rosendalsvägen 8, Ⓦ ullawinbladh.se.

"Ulla, my Ulla," goes the opening of a famous Swedish ballad by the eighteenth-century poet Carl Michael Bellman. The song is about his lover, Ulla Winbladh, and at this restaurant of the same name you can expect traditional Swedish home-cooked fare – think lots of seafood (particularly herring) and lingonberries. Inside there's an old-timey, farmhouse feel, with striped tablecloths, white wooden chairs and dark wooden pillars; outside, there's a gorgeous terrace for outdoor eating under red-striped awnings. KrKrKr

Villa Godthem

MAP PAGE 54, POCKET MAP G5
Rosendalsvägen 9, Ⓦ villagodthem.se.
Villa Godthem was built in 1874 as a private residence for local opera singer Carl Johan Uddman, before it was turned into an inn in 1897. Nowadays, this super-friendly restaurant is well-known for serving classic Swedish cuisine in a fantastic historical setting. One of their signature dishes is the steak, a real must-try for carnivores – but you can also come here for afternoon tea, a cute picnic menu of smaller plates and snacks, or a traditional Swedish crayfish party in August! KrKrKr

Blasieholmen & Skeppsholmen

Situated to the east of Gamla Stan, the islands of Blasieholmen and Skeppsholmen are places where you can steep yourself in Scandinavian art, architecture and design, as well as take some relaxing strolls with idyllic views. Now a peninsula between Norrmalm and Skeppsholmen, Blasieholmen is home to a number of elegant palaces built during the seventeenth and eighteenth centuries as well as to the Nationalmuseet, with the pretty Berzelli Park situated to the northeast. Across the bridge, Skeppsholmen, Stockholm's smallest island, was once a centre of naval architecture and a pleasant amble around it will reveal some key nautical sights; there are also three museums here that are really worth their salt.

Nationalmuseum

MAP PAGE 64, POCKET MAP D11
National Museum of Fine Art. Södra Blasieholmshamnen 2, Kungsträdgården T-bana, ⓦ nationalmuseum.se, charge; free for under-20s.

At the tip of Blasieholmen, the striking waterfront Nationalmuseum contains the largest art collection in all of Scandanavia. One of the world's oldest museums, it was founded in 1792 when it occupied a wing of the Royal Palace and was known as the Royal Museum. It moved to its current home, a massively impressive Italian Renaissance-style building, in 1866. Its doors were open without renovation or reprieve until 2013, when work

Skeppsholmen

Gallery 1920-1965, Nationalmuseum

began on a huge refurbishment that would take five years and over £100 million to complete. The thoroughly spruced up space reopened in 2018, proudly showcasing added exhibition space, a gorgeous courtyard on the ground floor full of stunning white marble sculptures and an incredible restaurant, as well as new lighting and ventilation systems designed to help protect and preserve the over five thousand works of art inside.

The collection, which includes Swedish and European fine and applied arts from the late medieval period to the present day, is contained over three floors. It is a truly remarkable collection, not only for its size but also for the scope of the paintings, sculptures, decorative arts, drawings and prints; among the old masters collection you'll find Rembrandts, plus important works by El Greco, Rubens, Goya and Brueghel, and a choice selection of Chardin oils. Courbet, Cézanne, Gauguin, Renoir and Manet are represented here, as are important Swedish artists, including Carl Larsson, Anders Zorn and Bruno Liljefors,

known for his vivid nature studies. Paintings to look for include François Boucher's *The Triumph of Venus*, considered his greatest work, and *The Lady and the Veil* by the Swedish painter Alexander Roslin (1718–93). In addition to these gems, there are thousands of prints, engravings and miniatures, more than two hundred Russian icons, and a selection of handicrafts to appreciate.

In 2023, environmental campaigners daubed red paint on Monet's *The Artist's Garden at Giverny*, which was on loan to the Nationalmuseum from the Musée d'Orsay in Paris. They then glued their hands to the frame as they chanted "our health is under threat" and "the climate situation is urgent". The organisation Återställ Våtmarker, meaning 'Restore the Wetlands', later claimed responsibility for the action; the painting was not damaged, and the climate crisis rolls on.

Skeppsholmsbron

MAP PAGE 64, POCKET MAP D12
One of Stockholm's most photogenic spots is

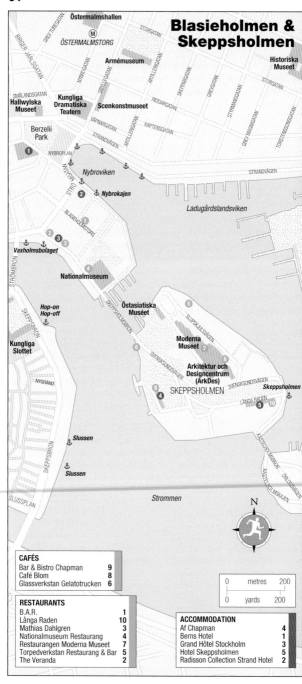

Blasieholmen & Skeppsholmen

CAFÉS
Bar & Bistro Chapman	9
Café Blom	8
Glassverkstan Gelatotrucken	6

RESTAURANTS
B.A.R.	1
Långa Raden	10
Mathias Dahlgren	3
Nationalmuseum Restaurang	4
Restaurangen Moderna Museet	7
Torpedverkstan Restaurang & Bar	5
The Veranda	2

ACCOMMODATION
Af Chapman	4
Berns Hotel	1
Grand Hôtel Stockholm	3
Hotel Skeppsholmen	5
Radisson Collection Strand Hotel	2

Skeppsholmsbron, the delightful wrought iron bridge that connects the island of Skeppsholmen to the city. At its midpoint, you'll find two gilded crowns, the symbol of Swedish royalty: one looks back into the city centre with spectacular views over the water, and the other faces the other way across to the greenery near Strandvägan. These views seem to sum up Stockholm perfectly: an urban cosmopolis with immediate access to magnificent natural landscapes.

Moderna Museet

MAP PAGE 64, POCKET MAP E12
Modern Art Museum. Exercisplan 2, Kungsträdgården T-bana, Ⓦ modernamuseet.se, charge; free for under 18s.

On Skeppsholmen itself, the Moderna Museet is one of the better modern and contemporary art collections in Europe; it's where Andy Warhol had his first-ever European exhibition. This fabulous building, designed by the prizewinning Spanish architect Rafael Moneo, was inaugurated in 1998 to celebrate Stockholm's

role as European City of Culture. You can download the museum's free app for direct access to an entire archive of over seventy recordings about some of the works on display. The museum's comprehensive selection of work is divided into three periods (1900–39, 1940–69 and 1970 to the present day) and comprises works by some of the twentieth century's leading artists, including Léger, Matisse, Braque, Modigliani, Klee and Rauschenberg, as well as by such notable Swedish artists as Isaac Grünewald and Bror Hjorth. Take a look at Dali's monumental *Enigma of William Tell*, showing the artist at his most conventionally unconventional, and Matisse's striking *Apollo*. Look out also for Picasso's *Guitar Player and Spring*, plus a whole host of works by Lichtenstein, Kandinsky, Miró, and Rauschenberg. The benefit of the museum's island location is best appreciated from its restaurant and café (see page 69), which afford wonderful waterside views thanks to generous floor-to-ceiling windows.

Moderna Museet

ArkDes, the Swedish Centre for Architecture and Design

Arkitektur och Designcentrum (ArkDes)

MAP PAGE 64, POCKET MAP E12
Architecture and Design Centre.
Exercisplan 4, Kungsträdgården T-bana,
Ⓦ arkdes.se, free.

Next door to Moderna Museet is Arkitektur och Designcentrum or ArkDes, which serves up a taste of Swedish architecture through the ages in one of the most inspired buildings in the city – there are lots of glass walls and bright, airy exhibition spaces. The permanent exhibition outlines some of the core themes of pan-Swedish architectural styles, and is housed alongside a number of temporary displays on construction styles. The collection guides visitors through a thousand years of Scandinavian building, from the simplest wooden houses to state-of-the-art techniques and styles, and the centre's archive contains 2 million drawings and sketches and six hundred thousand photographs – all of which are available for visitors to peruse. ArkDes is closed for restoration at the time of writing, but is due to reopen in summer 2024.

Östasiatiska Muséet

MAP PAGE 64, POCKET MAP D12–E12
Museum of Far Eastern Antiquities.
Skeppsholmen 41, Kungsträdgården
T-bana, Ⓦ ostasiatiskamuseet.se, charge;
free for under-19s.

A steep climb up the northern tip of Skeppsholmen brings you to the Östasiatiska Muséet, which is housed in a building dating from 1700 and was originally designed as a stable and quarters for Charles XII's bodyguards. A visit here is half a day well spent; you'll be rewarded by an array of objects displaying incredible craftsmanship, including many from China. In fact, its collection of ancient Chinese art is considered the best in the world outside of China, and includes eighteen hundred objects given to the museum in 1974 by the late King Gustaf VI Adolf, a distinguished archaeologist and a respected authority on Chinese art. The two main exhibitions, 'The Middle Kingdom' and 'China before China', tackle five thousand years of imperial Chinese history through a series of engaging artefacts, including just about anything you care to mention in

Fika: coffee and cake

Coffee is to the Swedes what tea is to the British, and you'll find sweets and pastries at almost every coffee shop, café and restaurant in Stockholm. This is because in Stockholm, and indeed all of Sweden, all activities and work are ceased twice per day at around 10am and 3pm in order to take 'fika' – a cup of coffee, accompanied by a pastry or piece of cake, more often than not in the form of a cinnamon bun (*kanelbullar*) or a cardamom bun (*kardemummabullar*). Coffee too is something the Swedes excel at, and is always freshly brewed, strong and delicious; unsurprisingly, then, Sweden is one of the world's nations that drinks the most coffee, even more than the Italians. Fika is a huge part of Swedish culture and says a lot about their holistic attitude to health and work; it's not just a sweet snack but functions as a social gathering, a break from work, a catch-up with colleagues, or even a first date. Some of Stockholm's biggest companies hold scheduled, company-wide fika breaks, and it's even been known to appear in job contracts!

porcelain. There are fifth-century Chinese tomb figurines, intricate ceramics from the seventh century onwards and fine Chinese paintings on paper and silk. Alongside these, are an astounding assembly of sixth century Buddhas, Indian watercolours, gleaming bronze Krishna figures and a magnificent set of samurai armour, a gift from the Japanese crown prince in the 1920s. The museum's stand-out exhibits include ancient Stone Age pottery, a reconstructed Chinese grave furnished with urns and axe heads grouped around a skeleton, colourful ceramics dating from the Ming Dynasty (1368–1644), and a series of impressive 3,000-year-old bronze sacrificial vessels.

Östasiatiska Muséet

Cafés

Bar & Bistro Chapman

MAP PAGE 64, POCKET MAP D12
Flaggmansvägen 8.
A cute little café with indoor and outdoor seating, the latter having magnificent views of the *af Chapman* schooner and over the water towards Gamla Stan. There's a good selection of hot drinks, lunches, pastries and other treats on offer, as well as a few alcoholic drinks. Perfect for a pit stop on a sunny afternoon after a walk or a stint at the museums. Kr

Café Blom

MAP PAGE 64, POCKET MAP E12
ArkDes, Exercisplan 4, Ⓦ cafeblom.se.
Located inside ArkDes, Café Blom serves delicious, healthy lunch dishes including salad bowls and sandwiches, as well as a few baked goods and very good coffee. During the summer, the tables outdoors are a lovely place to sit and relax; the cheerful yellow walls of ArkDes as well as the friendly service give everything a very feelgood atmosphere. If you're visiting in winter, the summery vibe is somewhat maintained by the lashings of natural light inside. Kr

Glassverkstan Gelatotrucken

MAP PAGE 64, POCKET MAP D12
Västra Brobänken, Ⓦ glassverkstan.se.
On the Skeppsholmen side of Skeppsholmsbron, you'll find the cute ice cream truck that is Glassverkstan Gelatotrucken. Selling handmade gelato made with all-natural ingredients (think fresh raspberries, pistachio puree, and lemon juice), the flavours are constantly changing depending on the season, availability of ingredients and the makers' moods. They also do a scrumptious vegan sorbet, and in 2023 added the outrageously popular waffle and gelato sandwich to the menu – velvety vanilla gelato sandwiched between warm waffles.

A real delight, and just a four-minute walk from their waterfront ice cream shop. Kr

Restaurants

B.A.R.

MAP PAGE 64, POCKET MAP D11
Blasieholmsgatan 4A, Kungsträdgården
T-bana, Ⓦ restaurangbar.se.
B.A.R. is *the* place to eat fish in Stockholm (even, arguably, in Sweden). Its bright and buzzy interior is reminiscent of an old fish market. Go up to the fish counter and choose the piece you'd like to eat; everything is delectable. There are also meat dishes on offer, including a tantalizing steak tartare. KrKrKrKr

Långa Raden

MAP PAGE 64, POCKET MAP E12
Gröna gången 1, Ⓦ hotelskeppsholmen.se.
Hotel Skeppsholmen's fantastic restaurant, Länga Raden, is an absolute must when you're visiting this gorgeous island, and is the only restaurant in the city that serves breakfast, lunch and dinner outside (providing the weather plays ball). The hotel enjoys a stunning waterfront location and has the feel of a real oasis of calm in the heart of the city. The menu is full of mouth-watering Swedish dishes made from fresh, seasonal ingredients (meatballs with lingonberry jam, anyone?). The prawns here also come highly recommended! KrKrKr

Mathias Dahlgren

MAP PAGE 64, POCKET MAP D11
Södra Blasieholmshamnen 8,
Ⓦ mathiasdahlgren.com.
Renowned master chef Mathias Dahlgren has been selected as the Swedish Chef of the Year no less than four times. He uses the best Swedish ingredients to create elegant, unusual, melt-in-the-mouth dishes in his two restaurants at the Grand Hôtel. Seafood Gastro focusses not just on fish, but also seabirds,

seaweed, coastal greens and anything else that lives in, by or on the water; note that they do not cater to vegetarians. The other restaurant, Matbaren, is a slightly more laidback affair, though still a real foodie find. The food is complemented by exceptional wines, most of which are served by the glass. The Green Rabbit bakery at Tegnérgatan 17 offers superb rye bread as well as breakfasts and soups. KrKrKrKr

Nationalmuseum Restaurang

MAP PAGE 64, POCKET MAP D11
Södra Blasieholmshamnen 2,
Ⓦ nationalmuseum.se.
The Nationalmuseum's restaurant was added as part of the huge restoration that took place between 2013 and 2018 with the idea that the food here should also be a work of art. The menu is made up of mouthwatering modern Swedish dishes containing ingredients that all come from Sweden – nothing is imported. And the food is only the beginning – as you might expect at a museum of fine art, everything in the restaurant has been designed with incredible care and attention, the result being that diners feel totally at relaxed and at ease – as if you're sitting in the living room of an old friend, even though in fact you're currently sat under stunning vaulted ceilings in rooms formerly used for storing artworks. KrKrKr

Restaurangen Moderna Museet

MAP PAGE 64, POCKET MAP E12
Exercisplan 2, Ⓦ modernamuseet.se.
Another ideal pitstop pre- or post-museum visit, the restaurant at the Moderna Museet serves lovely hot and cold lunches, salads, sandwiches and homemade cakes. With an outdoor terrace overlooking the water (naturally), this is a particularly inviting spot when the sun is out – but even if the weather isn't playing ball, the huge windows give great views regardless. There are

Nationalmuseum Restaurang

lots of tables which means it rarely feels overcrowded, and there are lots of vegetarian options. KrKr

Torpedverkstan Restaurang & Bar

MAP PAGE 64, POCKET MAP E12
Slupskjulsvägen 28, Ⓦ torpedverkstan.se.
For a little of that laidback archipelago ambiance in the middle of the city – Torpedverkstan Restaurang & Bar serves lunch, dinner, drinks and brunches, and features a really attractive seasonal menu with good meat, fish and veggie options. As with most Skeppsholmen restaurants, the weather can be the deciding factor in whether this place is good or great; it's particularly lovely if you're able to sit outside and enjoy the view of the boats bobbing in the water. KrKr

The Veranda

MAP PAGE 64, POCKET MAP D11
Södra Blaiseholmshamnen 8,
Ⓦ grandhotel.se.
No one should leave Stockholm without trying a smörgåsbord at this delightful restaurant in the Grand Hôtel, which looks out over the Royal Palace across the water. The dress code is smart casual. KrKrKrKr

Södermalm

Whatever you do in Stockholm, don't miss the delights of the city's southern island, Södermalm, whose craggy cliffs, turrets and towers rise high above the clogged traffic interchange at Slussen. The perched buildings seem vaguely forbidding, but venture beyond the main roads skirting the island and a lively and surprisingly green area unfolds, one that has, historically speaking, been working class at heart. Nowadays, it has been gentrified into the most youthful and bohemian island, earning itself the moniker 'the Brooklyn of Stockholm'. It's filled with art galleries, boutiques and clubs on top of many places of historic interest. After dark, you'll probably end up in one of Söder's bars or restaurants in the hip area known as SoFo; this is the handful of streets lined with cafés and restaurants which lie 'south of Folkungagatan' (hence the name), predominantly Åsögatan, Bondegatan and Skånegatan.

Fjällgatan

MAP PAGE 72, POCKET MAP E6-F6
Slussen T-bana.

Fjällgatan is where most of the city sightseeing buses stop. This little street, perched along the edge of a ridge overlooking the Baltic Sea, provides the visitor with one of the best panoramas of Stockholm. Not far from here there is a charming colony of shuttered, fenced-in cottages grouped on a grassy hill around the Sofia church.

Fotografiska

MAP PAGE 72, POCKET MAP E6-F6
Photographic Museum. Stora Tullhuset, Stadsgårdshamnen 22, Slussen T-bana, Ⓦ fotografiska.com/sto, charge; free for under-12s.

A mere five minutes' walk from Slussen along Stadsgårdsleden, the Fotografiska is one of the world's biggest galleries for modern photography. The gorgeous red-brick building is a former customs warehouse overlooking Stockholm's harbour; inside, the museum showcases the work of world-renowned photographers both in print and on film across three floors. Exhibitions change frequently, though there's every chance that one of the big names will be on display when you visit: star turns have included American Robert Mapplethorpe, France's Sarah Moon and Scottish photographer Albert Watson, whose work featured on over two hundred magazine covers, including Vogue. For unsurpassed views of the Stockholm waterfront, head up to the museum's top-floor café where the vistas are almost as breath-taking as the photographic work downstairs – and be sure to look out for the evening events here, which include talks and Q&As and often have live music.

Katarina kyrka

MAP PAGE 72, POCKET MAP E7
Högbergsgatan 13, Medborgarplatsen T-bana, free.

The Renaissance-style Katarina kyrka stands on the site where the victims of the so-called 'Stockholm Bloodbath' (see page 124) were buried in 1520. Though murderous and bloody, it proved a vicious and effective coup, as Christian disposed of the opposition in one fell swoop. In 1723, a devastating fire tore through the church, reducing it to ruins, an event that was repeated in 1990 when the building fell victim to another tragic blaze. Painstaking rebuilding work was finally completed five years later when the building reopened.

Systrarna (The Sisters)

MAP PAGE 72, POCKET MAP E6
Slussen T-bana.

A little to the west in a peaceful park, you'll find local sculptor Nils Sjögren's statue, *Systrarna* (*The Sisters*). The statue, which has been standing in Mosebacke Torg since 1945, depicts two nude women standing back-to-back, surrounded by a small body of water. The women's serene and relaxed expressions betray nothing of the statue's tragic backstory; the name of the statue is a little tongue-in-cheek, because the statue depicts two real women who were not sisters at all but rather lovers. Living in an era when same-sex love was not accepted or even tolerated, in 1911 the women tied themselves together and weighed themselves down with stones before drowning themselves in nearby Hammarby Sjö. If you visit Stockholm during the first week of August when Stockholm celebrates its annual Pride festival, you might well see a veil or a rainbow flag around their shoulders.

Katarinahissen

MAP PAGE 72, POCKET MAP E6
Slussen T-bana.

Slussen (the Sluice Gate) is a cloverleafed roundabout above

Södermalm

ACCOMMODATION
Clarion Hotel Stockholm	9
Hellstens Glashus	5
Långholmens Hotell	1
Den Röda Båten	2
Rival	3
Scandic Malmen	7
Skanstull's Hostel	8
Tre Små Rum	6
Zinkensdamm	4

Södermalm

the narrow canal connecting the lake with the sea. In the summer months, you'll see lots of pleasure boats lined up here waiting for the canal lock to be opened. Slussen is home, among other things, to one of the city's most curious sights: Katarinahissen (the Katarina Lift). Dating back to 1881, the 38-metre tall passenger lift rises in an open

The Girl With The Dragon Tattoo

In 2005, Steig Larsson's book *The Girl With The Dragon* tattoo was a runaway hit. It was followed up by two more novels to create a trilogy known as the Millennium books, as well as several films in Swedish; the English version of *The Girl With The Dragon Tattoo* stars Rooney Mara as the computer-hacker titular character, Lisbeth Salander, and Daniel Craig as the book's obsessive journalist protagonist, Mikael Blomkvist. The majority of the books' locations are found on Södermalm, some of which have become iconic for fans; Kaffebar, Blomkvist's favourite haunt, is based here, as well as *Kvarnen* (see page 80), where Salander hangs out with her bandmates. You'll also find Blomkvist's house on Bellmansgatan and Salander's opulent flat from the second book, *The Girl Who Played With Fire*, on Fiskargatan. Perhaps most excitingly for fans, *Mellqvist* coffee bar (see page 42), based in Vasastan, is reportedly where Larsson himself actually typed out many of the scenes that went into the book.

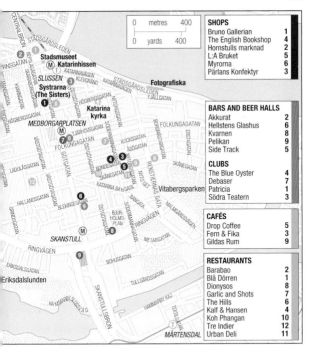

steel shaft to a pedestrian bridge which leads to the roof of a tall building, providing a welcome shortcut between Katarinavägen and Mosebacke Torg.

It stopped operating in 2010, but reopened in November 2023 so that visitors can once again enjoy gorgeous views over Gamla Stan and the water from the viewing platform at the top and from the lift itself as it ascends. A ten-minute walk east of here is Mariahissen, which is similar but less well-known; there was also once a lift here, but it closed in 1937. Today it's a lovely place to sit and drink a coffee while gazing out over Gamla Stan, and is relatively unknown except to locals.

Stadsmuseet

MAP PAGE 72, POCKET MAP D6
Stockholm City Museum.
Södermalmstorg, Slussen T-bana,
ⓦ stadsmuseum.stockholm, free.

In Södermalmstorg, right by the Slussen T-bana station, the rewarding Stadsmuséet houses collections relating to the city's history as a seaport and industrial centre. The Baroque building, designed by Tessin the Elder and finished by his son in 1685, was once the town hall for this part of Stockholm. Besides the museum, its most engaging offerings are the walking tours, which can be booked online. Among them are a tour of queer Stockholm and a guided walk around the old town. You can also buy maps in the gift shop that direct you on themed, self-guided routes. These include tours of Södermalm that allow you to follow in the footsteps of Lisbeth Salander and Mikael Blomkvist, the main characters of the Stieg Larsson Millennium novels (the most famous of which is *The Girl with the Dragon Tattoo*).

Katarina kyrka

Mariatorget

MAP PAGE 72, POCKET MAP D6
Mariatorget T-bana.

Södermalm's main square, Mariatorget, is a pleasant leafy space surrounded by grand Art Nouveau buildings on all sides. This is one of the most desirable places for Stockholmers to live, close to the stylish bars and restaurants that are the favourite haunts of Stockholm's young and terminally hip, in particular Benny Andersson's Rival hotel and bar (see page 111).

Hornsgatan

MAP PAGE 72, POCKET MAP B7–D6
Hornstull T-bana.

Hornsgatan, which begins with rows of art galleries in Slussen and ends at the water's edge in Hornstull, is lined with cafés, charity shops, vintage boutiques, and arts and crafts shops of all descriptions that showcase local artists. Check out the vibrant street market in Hornstull during the summer, filled with eclectic stalls and street performances (see page 75).

Långholmen

MAP PAGE 72, POCKET MAP A6–B6
True to its name ('long island'), Långholmen is a skinny sliver of land that lies off the north-western tip of Södermalm, crossed by the mighty Västerbron bridge linking Södermalm with Kungsholmen. To get there, take the T-bana or walk to Hornstull and then follow signs, or take bus #4, which crosses Västerbron on its way from Södermalm, Kungsholmen, Norrmalm and Östermalm. The water in Stockholm is clean and perfect for swimming during the long days of summer, and some of the best city beaches are located on Långholmen: there's family-friendly Långholmens Strandbad to the west of Västerbron bridge, and secluded and rocky Klippbadet to the east – this one is also a dog park, so be prepared to find yourself swimming with some furry friends! Leafy and peaceful, Långholmen is a delightful place to take a walk; on the way, you'll also get some stunning views of the city towards the Stadshuset and Gamla Stan.

Shops

Bruno Gallerian

MAP PAGE 72, POCKET MAP D7
Götgatan 36, Slussen T-bana,
Ⓦ brunogallerian.se.

Stockholm's smallest galleria is cute as a button, and somehow manages to retain the feel of a hidden gem, despite being located on the busy and bustling Götgatan. This shopping arcade is popular with locals and tourists, fashion and fika lovers alike; explore Swedish brands including Hope, & Other Stories, ARKET, Weekday and Monki. There's even a gym and a rooftop bar!

The English Bookshop

MAP PAGE 72, POCKET MAP E7
Södermannagatan 22, Skanstull T-bana,
Ⓦ bookshop.se.

There's no doubt you'll be learning a Swedish word or two on your visit to Stockholm, but for those who aren't quite fluent yet, the precious English Bookshop has you covered. A small shop that's brimming with books, you'll easily find a Swedish noir thriller or a collection of local recipes to take home as a souvenir you will actually use. This is a super cosy, independent store where the friendly staff are happy to chat, advise and make recommendations – and there's a good non-fiction section, too.

Hornstulls marknad

MAP PAGE 72, POCKET MAP A7
Hornstulls strand 4, Hornstull T-bana,
Ⓦ hornstullsmarknad.se.

During spring and summer, the promenade along the southwest edge of Södermalm island known as Hornstulls Strand hosts a flea market every weekend. It's absolutely packed with food trucks, antiques, vintage clothes, and stalls selling second-hand books, clothes, homewares, and records. There's also often a live band playing in good weather. A really great way to spend a couple of hours on a sunny afternoon, with a high chance of nabbing a pre-loved treasure.

L:A Bruket

MAP PAGE 72, POCKET MAP E7
Södermannagatan 19, Skanstull T-bana,
Ⓦ labruket.com.

Founded in Varberg on the west coast of Sweden, L:A Bruket is

Hornstulls marknad

a company that started out by making artisan soap. Today, they've branched out into skin lotions, shampoo, conditioner, and various other skincare products – even detergent. The focus here is on making quality skincare products from all-natural and sustainable ingredients, and if you're not convinced yet, the tempting aroma emanating from inside as you walk past will do the job!

Myrorna

MAP PAGE 72, POCKET MAP E7
Götgatan 79, Skanstull T-bana,
Ⓦ myrorna.se.

Myrorna is a chain of Swedish second-hand shops which is part of the Salvation Army. With branches all over Sweden, this two-storey spot in Södermalm has a surprisingly large section for non-clothing items including books and tableware – they always seem to have a lot of porcelain and glassware, and the quality is consistently high. The only downside is that it's so full to bursting with treasures that it can get a little crowded. There's another branch at Hornsgatan 96, which

Myrorna, Götgatan

has three floors and contains more clothes and home furnishings.

Pärlans Konfektyr

MAP PAGE 72, POCKET MAP E7
Nytorgsgatan 38, Skanstull T-bana,
Ⓦ parlanskonfektyr.se.

A glorious, cosy, old-timey sweet shop offering handmade caramels, fudge and chocolates. The fudge is particularly special, and comes in innovative flavours that you'd never have thought of – elderflower and blackcurrant, for example, or white chocolate and coconut. There's a production window through which you can see the delicacies being made, and they often have free samples on offer. They sell wildly popular ice cream here in summer, which comes in a huge range of flavours – all of which are delicious, so you really can't go wrong.

Cafés

Drop Coffee

MAP PAGE 72, POCKET MAP D7
Wollmar Yxkullsgatan 10, Mariatorget
T-bana, Ⓦ dropcoffee.com.

Barobao

An award-winning speciality coffee roastery run by true aficionados, this is one for the coffee nerds; the baristas here are friendly and really known their beans. All the coffee here is organic and fair-trade. This place has earned itself a bit of a cult following in recent times and so is often busy, but it's usually possible to find a spot to sit and enjoy a caffeine and cake break. Kr

Fern & Fika

MAP PAGE 72, POCKET MAP A6
Långholmsgatan 11, Hornstull T-bana,
Ⓦ fernandfika.com.

For those after a wholesome fika break, Fern & Fika delivers. With a plant-based menu from heaven, this little café is all about vegan, wholesome and extremely delicious food, all handmade in-house and presented to perfection. The pancakes are especially scrumptious! Stop off for breakfast, brunch, lunch, coffee or a sweet treat – given that it's all not just vegan but also mostly organic and local, it'd be rude not to. Kr

Gildas Rum

MAP PAGE 72, POCKET MAP E7
Skånegatan 79, Medborgarplatsen T-bana,
Ⓦ gildasrum.se.

A kitschy, old-timey café all done up in red and gold for an understatedly fabulous vibe. The bookshelf pattern on the wallpaper and the comfy armchairs lend this place the atmosphere of an old-fashioned reading room. There's a very popular array of baked goods as well as a great lunch menu, and there is outdoor seating for when the sun is shining. No wi-fi makes this a great spot for an undistracted catch-up or a peaceful hour with a coffee and a book. Kr

Restaurants

Barobao

MAP PAGE 72, POCKET MAP C6
Hornsgatan 66, Mariatorget T-bana,
Ⓦ barobao.se.

Decorated with hanging plants, this small, Asian-inspired restaurant serves beautifully soft steamed bao buns loaded with everything from pork belly to slow-cooked beef with green apple chutney. Innovative, trendy and affordable, Barabao offers healthy and organic fast food with a seasonal side-dish menu. No reservations. KrKr

Blå Dörren

MAP PAGE 72, POCKET MAP D6
Södermalmstorg 6, Slussen T-bana,
Ⓦ bla-dorren.se.

Unpretentious and popular beer hall-cum-restaurant with vaulted yellow ceilings offering excellent Swedish traditional dishes (such as elk meatballs, pickled herring, steak and pytt i panna) in good size portions. Great location for both Gamla Stan and Södermalm. KrKr

Dionysos

MAP PAGE 72, POCKET MAP E7
Bondegatan 56, Medborgarplatsen T-bana,
Ⓦ dionysos.se.

Tasteful Greek restaurant with a homely feel: it's been here since 1974, making it one of the oldest Greek restaurants in Stockholm, and is just as good as ever. The food is authentic and accomplished: menu highlights include the halloumi salad, *souvlaki* (meat skewers) and *biffteki* (mini burger patties). Portions are hearty; rest assured, you will not leave hungry. KrKrKr

Garlic and Shots

MAP PAGE 72, POCKET MAP E7
Folkungagatan 84, Medborgarplatsen
T-bana, Ⓦ garlicandshots.com.

A fun American-style diner where every dish is laced with garlic – you can ask for more garlic, but never less! Featuring an extensive, carnivore-pleasing menu including the likes of garlic and honey marinated pork belly and Transylvania vampire steak, there is also a vegan and veggie menu that's just as mouth-watering, graced by dishes including the seitan mixed grill as well as hot chili and garlic beans. There's also a wide-ranging choice of vodkas and aquavits – and even a garlic beer. There will be no kissing after this one! KrKr

The Hills

MAP PAGE 72, POCKET MAP D7
Götgatan 29, Slussen T-bana,
Ⓦ thehillsstockholm.se.

The Hills is an LGBTQ+-owned brasserie and trendy Stockholm hotspot that is a truly unmissable treat in the lively neighbourhood of Götgatsbacken. The Hills serves up mainly French food with Scandinavian influences

Gildas Rum

Dish at Blå Dörren

(the absolute stand-out dish from the menu is the lamb, which is transcendent), as well as a great wine list that features organic wines from all over the world. The Hills also does fantastic cocktails from a rotating menu – if you can't see one on the list, ask for something with punsch, a popular sweet Swedish liqueur. The interior is the work of famous Swedish designer Jonas Bohlin – and the toilets are an experience in and of themselves. Look out for the golden phallus hanging over one of the toilets, and be careful not to jump as a blank-faced mannequin stares out at you from the kitchen by the bathroom door. KrKrKr

Kalf & Hansen

MAP PAGE 72, POCKET MAP D6
Mariatorget 2, Mariatorget T-bana,
ⓦ kalfochhansen.se.
This tiny, casual place, run by a father and son team, specializes in organic fast food with a Nordic twist. Choose from fresh meat, fish and veggie options, served up with tasty sauces and seasonal vegetables and bread. The interior design matches the food in that it is simple and tasteful; a really good spot for lunch. Kr

Koh Phangan

MAP PAGE 72, POCKET MAP E7
Skånegatan 57, Medborgarplatsen T-bana,
ⓦ kohphangan.se.
A wacky, tropical-themed Thai restaurant that's playful and a whole lot of fun. The darkened interior is strewn with colourful fairy lights and is like a little slice of Thailand – there's even a tuk-tuk! The soups, salads and noodle dishes are all nicely done with a range of dishes to suit all spice tolerance levels. Listen out for the 'thunderstorm' that occasionally rumbles through the restaurant. KrKr

Tre Indier

MAP PAGE 72, POCKET MAP D7
Åsogatan 92, Medborgarplatsen T-bana.
A lively but unassuming Indian restaurant that's slightly tucked away; it's located at the corner of Åsögatan and the tiny street Möregatan. There's an extensive menu and the curry dishes are genuinely tasty and well prepared. Kr

Urban Deli

MAP PAGE 72, POCKET MAP E7

Nytorget 4, Medborgarplatsen T-bana, Ⓦurbandeli.se.

Urban Deli was first conceived of by a queer woman, and prides itself on being a humanity-positive concept store and restaurant that's incredibly popular; you're likely to see outlets all over Stockholm. The delis are always impressively well-stocked and the bistros chic and busy; at this branch, you'll find a handful of tables, plus stools at a long bar. It serves all meals, but especially good is the weekend brunch, which includes everything from fresh oysters to a classic Swedish fish stew. KrKr

Bars and beer halls

Akkurat

MAP PAGE 72, POCKET MAP D6

Hornsgatan 18, Slussen T-bana, Ⓦakkurat.se.

This famous spot is known for its 280 different whiskies and extensive beer selection on tap

and by the bottle, including an impressive array of Belgian varieties. Bartenders are knowledgeable and happy to advise, and there is often live music at weekends.

Hellstens Glashus

MAP PAGE 72, POCKET MAP D7

Wollmar Yxkullsgatan 13, Mariatorget T-bana, Ⓦhellstensglashus.se.

Relaxed chic is the name of the game at Hellstens Glashus. This boutique hotel is architecturally impressive, boasting exposed brick walls and a glorious multi-coloured glass façade that can be opened in summer to let in the breeze. It's an ideal spot for a chilled-out cocktail to begin the night; the bartenders are very friendly and happy to advise.

Kvarnen

MAP PAGE 72, POCKET MAP E7

Tjärhovsgatan 4, Medborgarplatsen T-bana, Ⓦkvarnen.com.

This legendary beer hall, with high ceilings and over a century's history, is a favourite haunt of football fans supporting Hammarby, who come here to celebrate their team's every win and defeat. There is also

Pelikan

a menu of great Swedish home cooking: reindeer is always on the menu, served with mushrooms and a creamy sauce. Kvarnen is also featured in Stieg Larsson's Millennium books as the meeting place for Lisbeth Salander and her bandmates.

Pelikan

MAP PAGE 72, POCKET MAP E8
Blekingegatan 40, Skanstull T-bana,
Ⓦ pelikan.se.

A long-established beer hall that's full of character – and characters – and is one of the city's most satisfying and relaxing places for an evening of drinking. Expect a cheerful, mixed crowd, high ceilings and a laidback atmosphere; it's a good place to strike up a conversation with local Swedes. There's also excellent traditional food on offer to the tune of meatballs 'as big as golf balls'.

Side Track

MAP PAGE 72, POCKET MAP D7
Wollmar Yxkullsgatan 7, Mariatorget
T-bana, Ⓦ sidetrack.nu.

This fun underground bar in Södermalm claims to be the oldest gay bar in Stockholm having opened its doors in 1998. Since then, it has garnered a good reputation for having no pretensions as well as for its pleasant staff, great food, and reliable music – a mixture of contemporary pop and classic bangers. A guaranteed good time.

Clubs

The Blue Oyster

MAP PAGE 72, POCKET MAP A7
Långholmsgatan 15, Hornstull T-bana,
Ⓦ instagram.com/theblueoysterstockholm.

Famous and friendly Stockholm gay bar with a dancey, club-type atmosphere later into the evening. This club plays mostly upbeat pop and dance tracks, and has outdoor seating in summer. Come for cocktails, drag queens, drag bingo and an all-round fun night out.

Debaser

MAP PAGE 72, POCKET MAP A7
Hornstulls Strand 9, Hornstull T-bana,
Ⓦ debaser.se.

Big-name DJs and live bands top the bill at this venue near the waterfront in Hornstull. They host a wide-ranging roster of events – expect anything from house to hip hop – but one thing that all events here have in common is a real love and admiration for music. There's also an American-style bar and a Mexican restaurant. The unusual lack of stairs in favour of ramps inside gives this place extra points for accessibility.

Patricia

MAP PAGE 72, POCKET MAP C6
Stadsgårdskajen, Slussen T-bana,
Ⓦ patricia.st.

What was formerly the royal yacht of Britain's late Queen Mother, the old ship Patricia today contains seven bars – two of which are outdoors – as well as a restaurant and a nightclub that plays chart and 1980s music, and a few schlager hits thrown in for good measure. The long-running Sunday club started 20 years ago and is still a very popular stop on Stockholm's gay scene. The restaurant's menu, with a huge variety of imaginative main courses (fajitas and Cajun steaks are always available) is quite simply terrific.

Södra Teatern

MAP PAGE 72, POCKET MAP E6
Mosebacke torg 3, Slussen T-bana,
Ⓦ sodrateatern.com.

One of the longest-established clubs in town; every night sees a different type of club or event taking place – expect everything from live music to club nights playing hip hop, indie rock or techno over three dancefloors. This is one of the best places in the capital for world music, hip-hop, rock and pop – if it's happening anywhere, it's happening here.

Östermalm

Blending into Norrmalm to the east, Östermalm is an affluent neighbourhood of stately apartment buildings and foreign embassies, whose grand, wide streets lend the area a distinctly upper-class feel. It's popular for its many antique shops and pricey boutiques, meaning that a bit of window shopping along its broad boulevards is an enjoyable way to pass an hour or two. There's also a huge park here, Humlegården, which is a lovely place to stretch your legs, or alternatively to take the opportunity to rest up a bit on the grass.

Hallwylska Museet

MAP PAGE 84, POCKET MAP D10
Hamngatan 4, Östermalmstorg T-bana,
ⓦ hallwylskamuseet.se, charge.

Just north of the pleasant Berzeli Park is the Hallwylska Museet. This patrician mansion, completed in 1898, was built for Walter and Wilhelmina von Hallwyl. He came from one of Europe's oldest noble families and she was the daughter of a steel and wood magnate. Wilhelmina was responsible for the amazing collections on display in the seventy perfectly preserved rooms, overflowing with Gobelin tapestries, china figurines, Flemish and Dutch paintings, antique furniture and assorted objects d'art. The mansion was surprisingly modern for the time, with electricity, central heating, hot and cold water, a bath and shower, and even indoor wood-panelled toilets. The Hallwyls donated the house to the state in 1920 and, after Walter's death in 1921, Wilhelmina left complex instructions in her will

Strandvägen, Östermalm

Kungliga biblioteket

(including the exact length – to the minute – of tours), as to how the museum was to be run after her death. She died in 1930 and the mansion remains more or less exactly as it was left.

Kungliga biblioteket

MAP PAGE 84, POCKET MAP D3
The Royal Library. Humlegårdsgatan 26, Östermalmstorg T-bana, Ⓦ kb.se, free.
Sweden's national library is tasked with preserving everything that is printed and published in Sweden – that's literally everything, whether a fashion magazine, film, schoolbook or radio news bulletin. Unsurprisingly, its vast archive stores over 18 million items, the oldest of which are a thousand years old. Known as KB for short, it has been located here since 1878, and is incredibly beautiful. You can visit for free, but be aware that you can't take much in with you – you'll be asked to leave all bags and coats behind before you enter. If you're not stopping by to work, remember to be quiet and respectful of those who are studying.

Östermalmshallen

MAP PAGE 84, POCKET MAP D10
Humlegårdsgatan 5, Östermalmstorg T-bana, Ⓦ ostermalmshallen.se.
Östermalmstorg is an elegant square that's home to the institution of Östermalmshallen, a wonderful indoor food market that's been decidedly popular ever since it opened in 1888. There are many different items sold here – you'll see lots of fresh fish, meat, sweets, and traditional Swedish delicacies including reindeer hearts and the wicked-smelling surströmming (fermented Baltic herring). The hall reopened in 2020 after renovations; a difficult time to reopen its doors perhaps, but today the market is thriving. Along with adding a number of new stores and traders to the mix, the renovations also reinstated the original star-shaped floor plan, and if you wander around its three floors at lunchtime you'll be sure to spot well-heeled ladies and gents sipping Chardonnay and munching on shrimp sandwiches. Perhaps you'll even join them?

Armémuseum

MAP PAGE 84, POCKET MAP D10
Army Museum. Riddargatan
13, Östermalmstorg T-bana,
Ⓦ armemuseum.se, charge; under-18s free.
Just beyond Östermalmshallen is the
Army Museum, which, while it may
not be to everyone's taste, does offer
a fascinating opportunity to learn
about Sweden's complex history in
terms of its military and warring
past. The museum tracks the
country's military history from the
sixteenth century to the present day,
with dramatic full-scale exhibitions
and fascinating trophy chamber.

Scenkonstmuseet

MAP PAGE 84, POCKET MAP D10
Swedish Museum of Performing Arts.
Sibyllegatan 2, Östermalmstorg T-bana,
Ⓦ scenkonstmuseet.se, charge; under-18s
free.
Heading around the corner into
Sibyllegatan will take you to the
Swedish Museum of Performing

Arts, which is devoted to dance,
music and theatre. This museum is
worth visiting even just to see the
old seventeenth-century Crown
Bakery that houses it. First opened
in 1901, the museum houses about
fifty thousand exhibits and is a
music lover's delight with a unique
collection of instruments, stage
models, costumes and puppets
among others. It's delightfully
interactive, and gives you the
chance to practice in a virtual
dance troupe, try on stage masks,
and create your own piece of music.

Kungliga Dramatiska Teatern

MAP PAGE 84, POCKET MAP D10
The Royal Dramatic Theatre. Nybroplan 2,
Östermalmstorg T-bana, Ⓦ dramaten.se.
Head to Nybroplan, a square at
the water's edge, and you'll be
confronted with the attractive
white-stone façade of the Kungliga
Dramatiska Teatern. This is

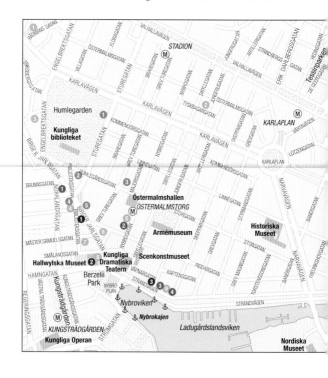

Scenkonstmuseet

Östermalm

BARS AND CLUBS
A Bar Called Gemma	3
Omnipollos Flora	1
Spy Bar	4
Sturehof	5
Terrace Bar	2

CAFÉS
Mr Cake	1
Saturnus	3
Triple Oh! Ice Cream	5

RESTAURANTS
East	4
Halv Grek Plus Turk	2
KB	8
PA & CO	6
Prinsen	7
T/bar	9

SHOPS
Acne Studios	2
Efva Attling	1
Svenskt Tenn	3

ACCOMMODATION
Hotel Diplomat	4
Hotel Esplanade	3
Hotel Kung Carl	1
Villa Dagmar	2

Stockholm's showpiece Royal Dramatic Theatre, and is more commonly known as Dramaten. It was here that the actors Greta Garbo, Ingrid Bergman and Max von Sydow all began their careers. Before his death in 1953, American playwright Eugene O'Neill bequeathed his last plays to the Dramatic Theatre, and their premieres (including that of *Long Day's Journey into Night*) were staged here. The theatre puts on a whopping one thousand shows every year across its five stages, and you can get a guided tour that takes you around the elegant marble foyer and the main stage, as well as snooping backstage at the costume department's extensive wardrobe. If you want to see a show, look out for performances which are subtitled in English.

Strandvägen

MAP PAGE 84, POCKET MAP D10–E11
Karlaplan T-bana.

The palatial houses along the fashionable quayside boulevard of Strandvägen (Shore Road) were built in the early twentieth century by Stockholm's ten richest citizens, seven of whom were wholesale merchants. This was a hilly, muddy harbour area until a campaign began in advance of the 1897 Stockholm Exhibition to create a grand avenue that was unrivalled in Europe at the time. Whether you choose to walk along the central promenade lined with linden trees or beside the quay where the old schooners are anchored, you'll find this is a pleasant stroll.

Historiska Museet

MAP PAGE 84, POCKET MAP E10
Museum of National Antiquities.
Narvavägen 13–17, Karlaplan T-bana,
Ⓦ historiska.se, charge; free for under-18s.

Towards the eastern end of Strandvägen, head north up Narvavägen to reach the impressive complex that houses the Historiska Museet. Covering a period of ten thousand years from the Stone Age to the Middle Ages, it is the most wide-ranging historical museum in Stockholm, with extensive displays of battles, beliefs and trading

Kungliga Dramatiska Teatern

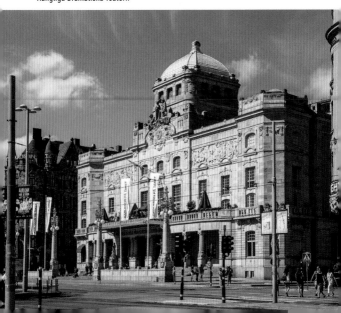

Historiska museet

patterns, and a breath-taking array of ornately decorated medieval triptychs from across the country. The 'door of history' at the main entrance, covered with allegorical and historical figures in bronze relief, is the work of the renowned Swedish sculptor, Bror Marklund. The museum has more than thirty rooms, so it's best to pick up a floor plan on your way in.

The section devoted to Sweden's Viking past is particularly engaging and informative in its efforts to portray Scandinavia's former inhabitants, not as warriors, but as farmers and tradesmen. Exhibits feature a magnificent 2.5m-high 'picture stone' from Gotland showing the entry of Viking warriors into Valhalla, as well as Sweden's best-preserved Viking-age boat, dated at around a thousand years old, discovered near Uppsala. There's also a lifelike model of the village of Birka, complete with an animated film showing daily life.

There are magnificent examples of medieval church art on the first floor, including wooden crucifixes modelled on Byzantine art, beautifully painted and sculptured altarpieces, baptismal fonts and gold chalices. One room is devoted entirely to a reconstruction of a typical medieval country church.

The museum's major attraction, though, is the Gold Room, located in a 'rock chamber' some 7m (23ft) below ground level in the museum garden. The circular room displays one of Europe's richest collections of prehistoric jewellery; with a magnificent 52kg of gold and 200kg of silver on show, including artefacts dating back as far as AD400, the Gold Room really steals the show. One of the collars is thought to have been worn by a king in the province of Västergötland and features seven rings superimposed on each other, all magnificently adorned with soldered figures.

An interactive exhibit at Tekniska museet

Sjöhistoriska Museet

MAP PAGE 84, POCKET MAP H4
National Maritime Museum.
Djurgårdsbrunnsvägen 24, bus 69 from
Nybroplan, Ⓦ sjohistoriska.se, charge;
under-18s free.

The National Maritime Museum
is found on the far eastern shore
of Östermalm. Located in a fine
building designed by Ragnar
Östberg, the same architect who
designed the Stadshuset, this
museum traces the history of
the Swedish Navy and merchant
marines from the seventeenth
century onwards. Here you'll
find over fifteen hundred mini
vessels and warships, and you'll
have the chance to learn about the
impact of merchant shipping on
Swedish society, life on deck and
shipbuilding – as well as, perhaps
more excitingly, about the lives
of pirates past and present! The
centrepiece of the collection is the
stern of the schooner Amphion,
which was instrumental in the
victory of a key battle against
the Russian Navy in 1790 under
the command of Gustav III,
and children will delight in the
playroom and frequent workshops.

Tekniska museet

MAP PAGE 84, POCKET MAP H4
Museum of Technology. Museivägen 7, bus
69 from Nybroplan, Ⓦ tekniskamuseet.se,
charge; under-7s free.

Tekniskamuseet is a sprawling
wonderland spread over five floors,
covering Swedish science and
technology through the ages in a
colourful, interactive way. There's
loads to do and see here – more
than enough to keep kids and
grown-ups alike entertained for
several hours, or even a whole
day. One of the more fascinating
attractions is a genuinely scary
reconstructed iron ore mine in the
building's basement, and another
is the Royal Model Chamber,
displaying the inventions of
Christopher Polhem (1661–1751),
a genius often described as the
'Father of Swedish Technology'.
There's also the Teknorama, a huge
room full of DIY experiments and
stations that test your flexibility,
balance and strength.

Shops

Acne Studios

MAP PAGE 84, POCKET MAP D10
Norrmalmstorg 2, Östermalmstorg T-bana,
W acnestudios.com.

High-end Swedish design brand
Acne Studios sells wildly expensive
but incredibly chic, high-quality
clothing and statement items for
men and women. The interior
is stunning, all white stone and
pillars; it's notable in and of itself,
as it used to be Kreditbanken,
the bank in which the infamous
Norrmalmstorg robbery took place
in 1973, from which the term
'Stockholm Syndrome' originates.

Efva Attling

MAP PAGE 84, POCKET MAP C10
Biblioteksgatan 14, Östermalmstorg
T-bana, W efvaattling.com.

Efva Attling is a former model
turned silversmith and jewellery
designer. She and her wife, pop
sensation Eva Dahlgren, are one of
Sweden's most well-known queer
power couples. Her collections
are known for mixing classic
Scandi simplicity with modernity,
resulting in classic pieces that feel
truly timeless whilst retaining their
humour and edge. Meryl Streep is
known to be a fan.

Svenskt Tenn

MAP PAGE 84, POCKET MAP D11
Strandvägen 5, Östermalmstorg T-bana,
W svenskttenn.com.

Walking into Svenskt Tenn is akin
to finding yourself in a delightful
museum – a real sweetshop for the
senses. This huge design store is full
of colourful furniture, homewares
and fabrics that will keep your eyes
busy for hours. The staff are happy
for you to have a look around even
if you don't buy anything – though
if you do decide to treat yourself,
you can be sure you're taking home
an item that you'll keep forever.
There's also a good café where you
can stop for a cup of tea.

Cafés

Mr Cake

MAP PAGE 84, POCKET MAP D3
Rådmansgatan 12A, Tekniska högskolan
T-bana, W mrcake.se.

The humourously-named Mr
Cake brings Americana to your
morning fika. This shop is packed
to the rafters with cinnamon rolls,
pastries, chocolates, popcorn, fresh
sandwiches and salads, and jaw-
droppingly beautiful cakes, all tied
up with pretty ribbons. The decor
is playful (and mostly pink). There's
good coffee here, too. Kr

Saturnus

MAP PAGE 84, POCKET MAP D3
Eriksbergsgatan 6, Rådmansgatan T-bana,
W cafesaturnus.se.

Saturnus is the place to come if you
like your coffee milky and served
in massive bowls, and your pastries
huge – the cinnamon rolls here
have been described by the Swedish
press as the best in town. Also
does good matcha lattes and hot
chocolates. It's warmly decorated
inside with a slightly Parisian feel.
Kr

Pastry at Saturnus

ÖSTERMALM

Triple Oh! Ice Cream

MAP PAGE 84, POCKET MAP D10

Nybrogatan 23, Östermalmstorg T-bana, Ⓦ ooo.se.

Having expanded from a small kiosk to Östermalm in 2022, Triple Oh!'s ambition is all in the name: it wants to create ice cream that makes you go oh, oh, oh'! Alongside the usual classics like vanilla, chocolate and pistachio, you'll also find a regularly changing selection of quirky flavours like strawberry and elderflower, baked apple, rhubarb rose, and whiskey. Kr

Restaurants

East

MAP PAGE 84, POCKET MAP C10

Stureplan 13, Östermalmstorg T-bana, Ⓦ east.se.

Trendy to a T, this is the place for top-quality cuisine from Japan, Korea, Thailand and Vietnam; try the delicious chicken soup with mushrooms, coconut, lime and

Prinsen

galangal. The food is top-notch and really worth the price. KrKrKr

Halv Grek Plus Turk

MAP PAGE 84, POCKET MAP E3

Jungfrugatan 33, Stadion T-bana, Ⓦ halvgrekplusturk.se.

Situated on a quiet corner, this friendly restaurant offers excellent value dishes from the eastern Mediterranean region. The generous 'chef's choice' meze sharing dishes are highly recommended, and will save you from having to make too many decisions. There are loads of veggie options too. With an understated, low-lit, relaxing interior, this place is perfect for a long, chatty dinner. KrKrKr

KB

MAP PAGE 84, POCKET MAP D10

Smålandsgatan 7, Östermalmstorg T-bana, Ⓦ konstnarsbaren.se.

Excellent Scandinavian food with plenty of seafood in classy 1930s surroundings, with walls full of art. The menu is based on simple dishes done really well; expect Swedish favourites and delicious seafood (fish stew or Norwegian cod) as well as some seasonal dishes. Come here for a very upscales (but not too stuffy) atmosphere at reasonable prices. KrKrKr.

PA & CO

MAP PAGE 84, POCKET MAP D10

Riddargatan 8, Östermalmstorg T-bana, Ⓦ instagram.com/p.a.co.restaurang.

This restaurant has earned a reputation for innovation that attracts many regulars and guests of local importance to savour its delicacies. Inside you'll find squashy leather sofas, chandeliers, marble-topped tables, candlelight and a convivial atmosphere. As for the menu, you can expect incredible steaks, delicious crab and, of course, meatballs. KrKrKr

Prinsen

MAP PAGE 84, POCKET MAP D10

Mäster Samuelsgatan 4, Östermalmstorg T-bana, Ⓦ restaurangprinsen.se.

A long-standing haunt of artists, musicians and writers enchanted by its soft lighting, ornate chandeliers, glass panelling and wall etchings, Prinsen has been going for over a hundred years. The food is top-notch Swedish home cooking, with the likes of wallenbergare (a Swedish veal dish), biff rydberg (beef, potatoes and onions) and herring all featuring prominently on the menu. Dinner is sometimes accompanied by live jazz. KrKrKr

T/bar

MAP PAGE 84, POCKET MAP D11
Strandvägen 7C, Östermalmstorg T-bana, Ⓦ diplomathotel.com.

A modern, stylish restaurant located on the ground floor of the Hotel Diplomat with views over the water. There's an interesting mixed menu ranging from club sandwiches to poached smögen cod with scampi, but always with a focus on locally sourced, globally-influenced Nordic cuisine. There's also a very good wine list. The restaurant is partnered with the World Childhood Foundation, meaning that if you eat meatballs here, a portion of the price is donated to charity. KrKrKr

Bars and clubs

A Bar Called Gemma

MAP PAGE 84, POCKET MAP E4
Grev Turegatan 30, Östermalmstorg T-bana, Ⓦ abarcalledgemma.se.

A Bar Called Gemma may not look like much, but step inside and you'll find an award-winning bar specialising in fancy cocktails. The bartenders here are highly skilled, clearly passionate, and experts at mixing innovative drinks – and if you can't decide, their signature cocktail (gin, sake, pistachio, ginger and citrus) is a solid bet. A fun and laidback spot.

Omnipollos Flora

MAP PAGE 84, POCKET MAP E3
Kungliga Humlegården 1, Stadion T-bana, Ⓦ omnipollosflora.com.

A lovely summertime spot in the serene greenery of Humlegärden, run by award-winning local brewers Omnipollo. With a good menu of burgers and ice cream with good plant-based options, the real stars of the show here are the craft beers and tropical pale ales. Really idyllic on a sunny day.

Spy Bar

MAP PAGE 84, POCKET MAP C10
Birger Jarlsgatan 20, Östermalmstorg T-bana, Ⓦ stureplansgruppen.se/nightlife/spy-bar.

Spy Bar in the heart of Stureplan is one of the competitors for the title of Stockholm's most famous nightclub. You'd do well to arrive early (around midnight, or even a little before) as it gets very busy and the queue can get unwieldy. Inside, the club is labyrinthine and there are always several DJs catering for a variety of tastes, with the atmosphere inside reaching a pinnacle at around 3am.

Sturehof

MAP PAGE 84, POCKET MAP D10
Stureplan 2, Östermalmstorg T-bana, Ⓦ sturehof.com.

This seafood restaurant has a fantastic and welcoming rooftop bar that gets very busy in summer, attracting a mixed crowd of all ages. Good beer and cocktails, but it's the wine list here that most people come for.

Terrace Bar

MAP PAGE 84, POCKET MAP E3
Humlegårdsgatan 23, Östermalmstorg T-bana, Ⓦ scandichotels.com/anglais.

On the seventh floor of the Scandic Anglais hotel, you'll find an incredible hidden terrace bar with wonderful views. Particularly good in summer when the sun is shining and there is a live DJ to accompany tasty cocktails made by knowledgeable bartenders.

Day trips

The loveliness of Stockholm's surroundings rivals the beauty of the city itself. To the east are the islands of the archipelago, and to the west is Lake Mälaren, with a collection of castles and towns at the water's edge. There are numerous boat excursions all summer long, on graceful old steamers or fast modern motor launches. Most of those heading for the archipelago will depart from either Strandvägen, across from the Royal Dramatic Theatre or Strömkajen, near the Grand Hôtel Stadshusbron, next to the City Hall, is the departure point for boats around Lake Mälaren. An hour or so north of Stockholm lies the vibrant university city of Uppsala, regarded as the historical and religious centre of the country, and attracting day-trippers seeking a lively alternative to Stockholm as well as travellers looking for a worthwhile stop on the long trek north.

Stockholm Archipelago

The Swedes call the Stockholm Archipelago Skärgården, which means 'garden of skerries', and it's a fitting description, a skerry being a small rocky reef or island. Huge and infinitely varied, this hauntingly beautiful archipelago consists of as many as thirty thousand islands of all shapes and sizes, extending for some 48km (30 miles) into the brackish waters of the Baltic. There is nothing like it anywhere else in the world.

In its day, the archipelago served as a place of refuge for pirates and smugglers. Later, fishermen lived in unpainted wooden shacks and wealthy noblemen built great estates on many of the islands. The archipelago has now become the favourite playground of Stockholmers that visit their summer holiday houses on weekends or for longer holidays, and they have a whale of a time sailing, fishing, swimming and sunning themselves on the smooth boulders by the water.

The archipelago is divided into three distinct sections, each with its own character and special atmosphere: the inner group is made up of larger islands covered with forests and farmland, the middle archipelago consists of a jumble of large and small islands, some with woods and fields of wildflowers, separated by a labyrinth of narrow channels and sounds, and the outer archipelago, mostly uninhabited, is a barren seascape of desolate rock islands.

Ekoparken

MAP PAGE 94
Ⓦ ekoparken.org.

Ekoparken is the world's first national city park, a huge set of green lungs which stretch out in a 12km (7mile) arch from Ulriksdals Slott (Ulriksdal Palace) in the north to the archipelago islands of Fjäderholmarna in the south, encompassing three royal parks, Djurgården, Haga and Ulriksdal. This green land is so large that you need a full day of serious hiking to explore it, by foot during the warmer months or on skis or long-distance skates in winter. A Royal Haga boat trip around the Brunnsviken is an excellent way to tour the Ekopark in summer (Ⓦstromma.se).

Vaxholm
MAP PAGE 94

Vaxholm is an attractive waterfront town in the inner archipelago popular with Stockholmers, reached by way of a charming 50-minute or so cruise aboard one of the boats operated by Ⓦaxholmsbolaget (Ⓦwaxholmsbolaget.se) or Cinderellabåtarna (Ⓦstromma.se). It's a charming place, with waterside paths and plenty of idyllic houses, cafés and restaurants; from the wooden harbour you can watch the motorboats and sailing boats manoeuvring through the narrow channel as they head for more distant points in the Stockholm archipelago. However, since all boats to and from Stockholm dock at Vaxholm, it's often swarming with visitors.

Vaxholm's chief attraction is the sixteenth century Fästnings Museet (Ⓦvaxholmsfastning.se); on a

little island guarding the straits by Vaxholm, this foreboding fortress once guarded the waterways into the city. Having successfully staved off attacks from the Danes and the Russians in its fortress days during the seventeenth and eighteenth centuries, it is now the National Museum of Coastal Defence.

Artipelag
MAP PAGE 94

Access via direct bus from Cityterminalen or passenger boat; see website for details, Ⓦartipelag.se, free; charge for exhibitions.
Opened in 2000, Artipelag is the brainchild of Björn Jakobson, the man behind the internationally renowned company Babybjörn. Located at Hålludden about 12 miles east of Stockholm (a 30-minute bus ride or a more scenic one-and-a-half-hour passenger boat journey), Artipelag is one for the foodies, nature-lovers, and those of an artistic persuasion. The name is a combination of the words art, activities and archipelago, which says a lot about what you can expect from this art gallery and nature park, but it doesn't tell the whole story. The complex is set

Vaxholm Fortress

DAY TRIPS

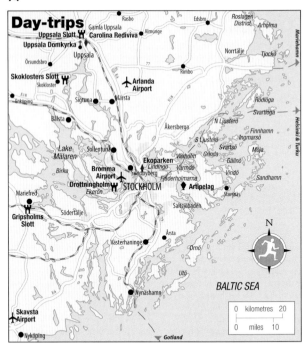

Day-trips

Rasbo · Edsbro · Roslagen District · Arholma

Uppsala Slott · Gamla Uppsala · Carolina Rediviva · Almunge

Uppsala Domkyrka

Örsundsbro · Uppsala

Skoklosters Slott · Skokloster

Enköping · Sigtuna · Märsta

Arlanda Airport

Bålsta · Åkersberga

N Ljusterö

Lake Mälaren · Sollentuna

Ekoparken

Birka

Bromma Airport · Lidingö · Sundbyberg

Drottningholm · STOCKHOLM · Artipelag

Ekerön · Fjäderholmarna

Mariefred · Södertälje · Saltsjöbaden · Stavsnäs

Gripsholms Slott

Årsta

Vasterhaninge · Ornö

Utö

Nynäshamn · BALTIC SEA

Skavsta Airport

Nyköping · Gotland

Norrtälje · Tjockö

Rimbo · Rödlöga · Svartlöga

S Ljusterö · Finnhamn · Ingmarsö · Svartsö · Grinda · Möja · Gällnö · Värmdö · Vindö · Sandhamn

N

Mariehamn · Helsinki & Turku

0 kilometres 20
0 miles 10

in 54 acres of beautiful waterside woodland, with amazing views over Baggen's Bay and relaxing nature walks, all accessible by wooden walkways. The building itself is something of an architectural marvel; architect Johan Nyrén was inspired by the four elements of earth, air, fire and water, and the building features all four in some manner or other. Be sure to seek out the plant-covered roof where herbs and vegetables to be used in the restaurant are growing, and the huge rock (or 'båda') that rises up out of the floor in the café; it's two billion years old.

Artipelag hosts boundary-crossing art exhibits across its four exhibition spaces, and also includes an events venue called Artbox where various opera performances and TV recordings take place. There are two restaurants here, both with outdoor seating and accompanying magnificent views.

Be sure to stop for fika at *Bådan Café*, where pastry chef Annie Hesselstad is known for creating 2022's Nobel Banquet dessert – and, well, if it's good enough for Nobel Prize winners…! Finally, don't miss the toilets on the ground floor; with their stone walls and communal sink made from a huge rock, they are something of an art exhibition in and of themselves.

Sandhamn
MAP PAGE 94

Sandhamn is located on a Baltic island at the outer edge of the archipelago. The fastest way there is on a Cinderella Båtarna vessel, which takes 2.25 hours from Strandvägen. There is a restaurant/bar on board, meaning you're able to take in all the diverse and dramatic elements that make up this stunning island world with a good meal in your belly and a drink in your hand.

The crayfish party

A delightful custom not to be missed by anyone visiting Sweden in August is the kräftskiva, or crayfish party. This is a traditional summertime food celebration, when Swedes abandon all rules of table etiquette as they attack mounds of small lobster-like creatures gleaming bright red in the light from the paper lanterns strung above the tables. Kryddost (spiced cheese), buttered toast and fresh berries complete the traditional menu. The mood becomes more and more festive as liberal amounts of aquavit are downed; it's also customary to don kitschy paper hats and protect the tables with tablecloths and your clothes with bibs, as crayfish shell and meat starts to fly everywhere when the party really gets going. Each dram of aquavit is accompanied by a bouncy snapsvisa, or drinking song – a particular favourite is the extremely jolly Helan Går, which, rather fittingly, roughly translates to "down in one".

With its fine harbour, the island of Sandhamn has been a destination for seafarers since the eighteenth century and remains so today, attracting yachts of all shapes and sizes; it is the home of the fashionable Royal Swedish Yacht Club. The tiny, charming village is a haven of narrow alleyways, winding streets and overgrown verandas, with only about a hundred year-round residents – but that figure swells in the summer when tourists and Stockholmers who have summer holiday cottages here invade the island. If you fancy staying overnight there are a couple of good options (see page 112).

Fjäderholmarna
MAP PAGE 94

If you prefer not to venture so far into the archipelago, then a trip to Stockholm's closest cluster of archipelago islands, Fjäderholmarna ('Feather Islands'), could be right up your proverbial street; at just 30

Artipelag

Beach on Mariehamn

minutes away by boat, you could pop over for as little as half a day if you're pressed for time. The main island of Stora Fjäderholmen is made up of quaint streets that are full of restaurants, bars, breweries and even a handicraft village of independent shops and artists' studios; wander round here and you'll find all kinds of treasures, from handcrafted pottery and jewellery to homemade sweets and chocolate. This is also the location of a delightful waterfront fish smokery and restaurant called *Rökeriet* (restaurangrokeriet.se), which is housed in a red warehouse standing at the north of the harbour. It's renowned for its excellent menu of salmon, mackerel and Baltic herring, and is a great place for a crayfish party if you have the good fortune to be visiting in August (see page 95). Fjäderholmslinjen operates frequent sailings to Fjäderholmarna from Slussen as well as Stromma from Nybroplan (stromma.se).

Mariehamn

MAP PAGE 94

Another fine outing is a cruise to Mariehamn, the capital of the Åland islands, comprised of 9,970 sq km (3,850 sq miles) of bays, inlets, islands and skerries located about midway between Sweden and Finland. This autonomous province of Finland has a population of twenty-five thousand, most of whom also speak Swedish. An overnight stop is preferable, though day cruises leave in the morning, stop for a couple of hours in Mariehamn, and are back in Stockholm by late evening, so you could do it in a day if you wanted to. You can also take a 24-hour excursion, sleeping onboard in a comfortable cabin or spending the night in a hotel in Mariehamn. The town has good accommodation facilities and some excellent restaurants. For more details, contact the Åland Tourism Board (visitaland.com).

Lake Mälaren

Freshwater Lake Mälaren is Sweden's third largest lake, stretching more than 110km (68 miles) west of Stockholm. This area, the Lake Mälaren Valley, has been justly termed the cradle of Swedish civilisation and its most important historic sights are within easy travelling distance from Stockholm via waterways.

Drottningholm

MAP PAGE 94

ⓦ **kungligaslotten.se.**

Even if your time in Stockholm is limited, an excursion to Drottningholm deserves a place on your itinerary. Beautifully located on the shores of leafy Lovön, an island 11km (7 miles) west of Stockholm's centre, it takes less than an hour to reach. Whereas the Royal Palace in Stockholm's city centre is a stately, square affair, Drottningholm is more reminiscent of fairy tales and Disney princesses, with huge, manicured lawns and a sweeping pale yellow façade. It is perhaps the greatest achievement of the two architects Tessin, father and son. Work began in 1662 on the orders of King Karl X's widow, Eleonora, with Tessin the Elder modelling the new palace in a thoroughly French style – giving rise to the stock comparisons with Versailles. Apart from anything else, it's considerably smaller than its French contemporary, utilizing false perspective and trompe l'oeil

to bolster the elegant, though rather narrow, interior. On Tessin the Elder's death in 1681, the palace was completed by his son, then already at work on Stockholm's Kungliga Slottet.

Since 1981, the Swedish royal family has lived out at Drottningholm instead of in the city centre, using it as a permanent home; they live in the south wing, which is not open to the public. This move accelerated efforts to restore parts of the palace to their original appearance, and the monumental grand staircase is now once again exactly as envisaged by Tessin the Elder. In the rooms, good English notes are available to help you sort out the riot of Rococo decoration, which largely dates from the time when Drottningholm was bestowed as a wedding gift on Princess Louisa Ulrika (a sister of Frederick the Great of Prussia).

No hints, however, are needed to spot the influences in the Baroque 'French' and the later 'English' gardens that back onto the palace. Within the extensive palace grounds is the Kina Slott (Chinese Pavilion), a sort of eighteenth-century royal

Drottningholm

summerhouse that displays an unusual combination of the Rococo and Chinese styles with its two curved wings. It was originally built by King Adolf Fredrik as a birthday gift to Queen Louisa Ulrika in 1753, at a time when no one had any real idea of what a Chinese Pavilion should look like. Very close to it is the even more unusual Guard's Tent. It does look just like a tent, but a closeup look tells quite a different story; in fact, it was built in 1781 to serve as quarters for the dragoons of Gustav III, and the intent was to make it look like a "tent in a Turkish army camp".

The Drottningholm Court Theatre is adjacent to the palace and is one of the world's most famous theatrical establishments. Not content with this theatre, King Gustav III also constructed a small castle theatre at Gripsholm Slott in the same era. During the summer, this gem of a theatre is the venue for operas by Handel, Gluck, Mozart and others, as well as ballet. The additional touch of musicians dressed up in authentic period costumes and wearing powdered wigs makes you feel as if you're attending a court entertainment

some two hundred years ago. Before or after the performance, take the opportunity to look at the collections of pictures and costumes tracing the history of stage art, exhibited in the rooms around the auditorium. They include rare Italian and French theatrical designs from the sixteenth to eighteenth century and original sketches by Gustav III's stage painter. Even if you can't make a performance, a guided tour is a must.

Birka

MAP PAGE 94

The island of Björkö (the name means "island of birches"), is the site of Sweden's oldest town, Birka, which was founded around 750AD and is now a UNESCO World Heritage site; you can get here from the city in just under two hours. For over two centuries, Birka was the most important Viking trading centre in the northern countries, benefiting from its strategic location near the mouth of Lake Mälaren on the portage route to Russia and the Byzantine Empire. Birka reached its peak during the tenth century before sliding into decline: falling water levels in Lake Mälaren, the

Boats at Birka

Gripsholm

superior location of the Baltic island of Gotland for handling Russian–Byzantine trade and the emergence of rival Sigtuna all led to its gradual disappearance after 975.

Today, a visit here presents an opportunity to get to grips with Sweden's Viking heritage, thanks to the site's excellent museum. Major excavations began on the island in 1990 and the Birka museum now recounts the village's history in superb detail. Exhibitions explain how, during Viking times, Björkö was actually two separate islands. As the land rose after the last Ice Age, the narrow channel between the two islands vanished, resulting in today's single kidney-shaped island. Displays of historical artefacts as well as scale models of the harbour and craftsmen's quarters are also available for perusal. The developed nature of Viking society is evident from the finds: scissors, pottery and even keys have all been excavated. In addition to the museum, it's possible to stroll around a reconstruction of a Viking village for a taste of how things once looked. In July you can even come face to face with modern-day Vikings, when the staff don period costumes and enact Viking games. Among Birka's Viking remains, though, the most striking is the island's graveyard, which is the largest Viking-age burial ground in Scandinavia with around four hundred burial mounds, some accompanied by standing stones.

Gripsholm Slott
MAP PAGE 94
Ⓦ kungligaslotten.se.

A site that justifies a full day's excursion is Gripsholm Castle. You can be there in an hour and a half by train to Läggesta followed by a short bus ride, but an alternative route by boat is a far more pleasing proposition. The SS Mariefred (Ⓦ mariefred.info) is a coalfired steamer that has been plying the same route since 1903. It makes for a highly memorable trip and you can even enjoy dinner on board. It departs from Stadshusbron in the morning and returns from Mariefred in the late afternoon, with each trip taking 3.5 hours.

At journey's end you'll see the imposing, turreted bulk of Gripsholm Slott, mirrored like a stage set in the waters of the lake. There was a castle on this site in the

1300s, built by the great Bo Jonsson Grip, but the present structure was built by Gustav Vasa in the 1530s. Now a museum, Gripsholm houses one of the largest collections of historical portraits in the world. Don't miss the small castle theatre built by Gustav III (who was also responsible for the Drottningholm Theatre); it's too delicate to be used for performances these days, but in summer, plays and other events are staged out in the castle grounds. Even ABBA have put in an appearance here – in February 1974, Gripsholm was used as the cover shot for their Waterloo album.

Next door to the castle is Mariefred; you might want to pause a while in this attractive little town of yellow and red frame houses, with lovely gardens lined up in tight rows beside narrow streets and a cobblestone square. A white baroque church and an eighteenth-century town hall are two of the highlights here. Before leaving Mariefred you should take a ride on the Östra Södermanlands Järnväg, a rolling museum of vintage coaches pulled by an old steam engine. This narrow-gauge railway, which dates from 1895, is maintained by local rail buffs. It runs from Mariefred to Läggesta,

Stora Gatan, Sigtuna

a distance of 4km (2.5 miles). At a top speed of 25km/h (12mph), it's a slow but delightful trip.

Sigtuna

MAP PAGE 94

Sigtuna is a compact little town situated on a beautiful, slender arm of the lake; it dates all the way back to Viking times, with extensive ruined churches and rune stones right in the centre. It is thought to be Sweden's oldest existing town, having been founded in 980 by King Erik Segersäll. It served as the religious centre of the country – a role later taken over by Uppsala – and is the site of some of Sweden's oldest churches. It was also Sweden's first capital and a lively trading port until pirates burned it to the ground; the town gradually recovered, but Gustav Vasa, fired up by the ideas of the Reformation, shut down its monasteries and the town fell into obscurity.

Walk along Stora Gatan, which is said to be the oldest street in Sweden; the original, laid out during the king's reign, still lies under its modern-day counterpart. You'll find the quaint town hall on this street, as well as two of Sigtuna's most impressive ruins, the churches of St Per and St Olof. Much of the west and central towers of St Per's still remain from the early 1100s; experts believe it likely that the church functioned as a cathedral until the diocese was moved to nearby Uppsala. The unusual formation of the vault in the central tower was influenced by church design then current in England and Normandy. Further east, St Olof's has impressively thick walls and a short nave, the latter suggesting that the church was never completed. Close by is the very much functioning Mariakyrkan, constructed of red brick during the mid-thirteenth century to serve the local Dominican monastery. Inside, the walls and ceiling are richly adorned

Skoklosters

with restored paintings from the fourteenth and fifteenth centuries.

Another point of interest, aside from scattered rune stones from the Viking era, is the Sigtuna Museum (Ⓦ sigtunamuseum.se), which contains local archaeological finds including coins, gold rings and even an eleventh-century clay egg from Kiev.

Skoklosters Slott

MAP PAGE 94

Skoklosters Slott (Ⓦ skoklostersslott. se) is a magnificent baroque palace on the edge of a lovely bay on Lake Mälaren, about 20km (12 miles) northeast of Sigtuna. It was constructed in the latter part of the seventeenth century by Carl Gustaf Wrangel, a field marshal under Gustavus Adolphus in the Thirty Years' War. The castle's one hundred oversized rooms house a fabulous collection of historical treasures, mostly from the seventeenth century when Sweden was Europe's preeminent military power. The collection includes silver and glass pieces, tapestries, baroque furniture, over a thousand paintings and twenty thousand rare books and manuscripts, much of it war booty. The arms collection, one of the largest in the world, begins with crossbows and includes such oddities as a set of executioner's swords and a 2.5m (8ft) long rifle that belonged to Queen Christina (see page 24).

Uppsala

Uppsala, population 150,000, is 73km (45 miles) north of Stockholm and can be reached in under an hour by train or in an hour and fifteen minutes by bus, both from Centralstationen. This excursion more than justifies an overnight stop. History jostles you at virtually every corner in Uppsala, an ancient centre of culture, religion and education. It's the seat of the Archbishop of the Swedish Church and home of Uppsala University, one of the world's great institutions of higher learning, which celebrated its 500th anniversary in 1977. It also has a charming atmosphere, with the Fyrisån River meandering its way through the centre of town, a green patina forming on the campus statues, rare and beautiful flowers blooming in the Linnaeus

Gardens, and the old wooden buildings ageing gracefully and in sharp contrast to the new glass and steel structures. Most distinctive of all is Uppsala's skyline silhouette; the twin spires of the cathedral and the round towers of the castle are both centuries-old landmarks that dominate the city.

Uppsala Domkyrka

MAP PAGE 94
Uppsala Cathedral. Ⓦ svenskakyrkan.se/
uppsaladomkyrka, free.

Begin your sightseeing at Uppsala Domkyrka, right in the middle of the university grounds. This massive thirteenth-century cathedral is the largest in northern Europe, with its lofty 122m (400ft) spires; it took over 150 years to build. Many famous Swedes are buried here: King Gustav Vasa (and his three wives); St Erik – Sweden's patron saint and king who died a martyr in Uppsala in 1160; Emanuel Swedenborg, mystic, scientist and philosopher; and Carl Linnaeus, the botanist who, like Swedenborg, worked at Uppsala University. The Treasury Tower Museum contains religious tapestries, articles of silver and gold and other objects of great historical and aesthetic interest. Before you leave, pause to look at the medieval wall paintings in the Trinity Church,

which dates back to the 1300s. Close by is the *Domtrappkällaren* restaurant (Ⓦ domtrappkallaren.se), set in a fourteenth-century cellar and serving Swedish cuisine with international touches; specialities include delicious salmon and reindeer, as well as other fresh game dishes.

Uppsala Slott

MAP PAGE 94
Uppsala Castle. Ⓦ uppsalaslott.com, charge.

Construction of this looming red structure on a hill overlooking the town began in the 1540s under Gustav Vasa. The castle has been the setting of lavish coronation feasts and many dramatic historic events. It was here, for instance, that Gustavus Adolphus held the talks that led Sweden into the Thirty Years' War, and that Queen Christina gave up her crown in 1654 before setting off for Rome (see page 24). Today Uppsala Castle is home to the Uppsala Konstmuseum, which exhibits contemporary art.

Carolina Rediviva

MAP PAGE 94
Ⓦ ub.uu.se, free.

Carolina Rediviva is perhaps the most notable of the university buildings, as it houses the biggest

Swan pond and Uppsala Castle

and oldest library in Sweden, founded by Gustavus Adolphus in the seventeenth century. The collection contains 5 million books and half a million manuscripts and documents, many from medieval times. Among them are extremely rare items, including the Codex Argenteus (Gothic Silver Bible), written in the sixth century in silver letters and gold capitals on purple parchment.

Gustavianum

MAP PAGE 94

Ⓦ gustavianum.uu.se, free.

The Gustavianum is another university building, this one topped by a most curious room: an octagonal anatomical theatre under a striking dome. It was built in the 1620s by Olof Rudbeck, one of many brilliant scientists who have taught and conducted research here. Now home to the University Museum, it contains an exhibit on early anatomical and medical studies, Nordic and Egyptian antiquities and – a real gem – the thermometer of Anders Celsius.

Linnéträdgården

MAP PAGE 94

Ⓦ botan.uu.se, charge.

Many people travel to Uppsala simply to visit places connected with Carl Linnaeus, famous as the 'Father of Modern Botany'. Linnaeus came to Uppsala in 1728 as a medical student, was appointed lecturer in botany after only two years at the university, and became a professor of medicine in 1741. Linnaeus named and described some ten thosand different species of plant. Some of these species can be seen in the university's Linnéträdgården, which houses thirteen hundred plants arranged according to species, exactly as in Linnaeus's era. His home in the gardens is now a museum and is open to the public. During the summer, botanists lead groups of visitors on marked trail walks following the

Botaniska Trädgården

footsteps of Linnaeus in the forests around Uppsala.

Botaniska Trädgården

MAP PAGE 94

Ⓦ botan.uu.se.

Another one for those with interests of a botanical nature, the Botaniska Trädgården is a must-see. Over thirteen thousand different species and subspecies from around the world are found here, including tropical plants, and Mediterranean trees and shrubs in the Tropical Greenhouse and Orangery.

Gamla Uppsala

MAP PAGE 94

Gamla Uppsala (Old Uppsala) is about 3km (2 miles) out of town and can be reached by bus from the city centre. This is the site of the ruins of a pagan temple and three huge burial mounds said to contain the remains of kings mentioned in the epic Beowulf. The graves, dating from the sixth century, are called Kungshögarna (Kings' Hills). A twelfth-century parish church stands on the remnants of the heathen temple where human and animal sacrifices were offered up to the gods. Close by is *Odinsborg* restaurant and café (Ⓦ odinsborg. nu), where you can drink mead (*mjöd*) from old Viking oxhorns.

ACCOMMODATION

Hôtel Reisen

Accommodation

Stockholm has plenty of accommodation to suit every taste and pocket, from elegant upmarket hotels with waterfront views to youth hostels in unusual places – two are on boats and another is in a former prison. The cheapest choices on the whole are found to the north of Cityterminalen, but don't rule out the more expensive places; there are some attractive weekend and summer prices that make a spot of luxury nearer the waterfront a little more affordable.

Gamla Stan

HÔTEL REISEN MAP PAGE 26, POCKET MAP D12. Skeppsbron 12, ⓦ hyatt.com/en-US/hotel/sweden/hotel-reisen/arnub; Gamla Stan or Slussen T-bana. One of Stockholm's classic hotels, this nicely located and beautifully designed hotel dates back to the eighteenth century. Rooms are decked out with handsome wood panelling and Swedish antiques, and all have bathtubs, which is not the norm in Sweden. The more expensive options even have their own Jacuzzis, saunas and balconies overlooking the waterfront. There's also a pool and a sophisticated piano bar. KrKrKrKr

LADY HAMILTON HOTEL MAP PAGE 26, POCKET MAP C12. Storkyrkobrinken 5, ⓦ thecollectorshotels.se/lady-hamilton; Gamla Stan T-bana. This Class-A listed building dates from the late fifteenth century. Expect nautical memorabilia and antiques – including a large collection of stately grandfather clocks. A particularly unique feature of this place is that you can take a dip in an early fourteenth-century well in the basement, should you so desire! KrKrKr

LORD NELSON MAP PAGE 26, POCKET MAP C12. Västerlånggatan 22, ⓦ lordnelsonhotel.se; Gamla Stan T-bana. The sister hotel to the Lady Hamilton, this seventeenth-century building is one of the narrowest hotels in Sweden at just 5m (16ft) wide. It's stuffed full of naval antiques and curiosities including an original letter from Nelson to Lady Hamilton. Rooms are cosy, with ship's teak floorboards and lots of mahogany and brass for a continuing nautical flavour. Overall, a friendly and intimate place to stay. KrKrKr

MÄLARDROTTNINGEN MAP PAGE 26, POCKET MAP B12. Riddarholmen, ⓦ malardrottningen.se; Gamla Stan T-bana. One of Stockholm's most unusual hotels, this is a 1920s luxury yacht moored off the island of Riddarholmen, right next to Gamla Stan. The elegant white ship

Accommodation price codes

The price categories below are based on two people sharing a double room at full rates, including breakfast, Moms (sales tax at 12 percent for accommodation), and service charge. However, there are usually substantial discounts for weekends and during the summer season.

Kr – below 1,000 kr
KrKr – 1,000–1,500 kr
KrKrKr – 1,500–2,200kr
KrKrKrKr – over 2,200kr

was formerly the gin palace of American millionairess Barbara Hutton, and its cabins have been converted into hotel rooms; they're a little cramped perhaps, but make a fun change nonetheless. KrKrKr

SCANDIC GAMLA STAN MAP PAGE 26, POCKET MAP C13. Lilla Nygatan 25, Ⓦ scandichotels.com; Gamla Stan T-bana. A converted seventeenth-century house at the southern end of the Gamla Stan. Quiet and tucked away among the narrow streets, all rooms have been renovated to a high standard in an eighteenth-century Gustavian style. KrKrKr

SVEN VINTAPPARE MAP PAGE 26, POCKET MAP C12. Sven Vintappares Gränd 3, Ⓦ hotelsvenvintappare.se; Gamla Stan T-bana. Housed in a charming building from 1607 with just seven rooms, all of which are decorated in Swedish Gustavian style. The bathrooms are to die for, their granite floors and marble walls completing the sense of royal elegance. KrKrKr

VICTORY HOTEL MAP PAGE 26, POCKET MAP C12. Lilla Nygatan 5, Ⓦ thecollectorshotels.se/en/victory-hotel; Gamla Stan T-bana. This seventeenth-century residence in Gamla Stan is now a small, intimate hotel, named after Lord Nelson's flagship. The rooms individually are all decorated with antique furniture, and there's a relaxed bar, a sauna and an excellent restaurant. KrKrKr

Norrmalm & Vasastan

BEMA MAP PAGE 36, POCKET MAP C3. Upplandsgatan 13, Ⓦ bema.hotels-stockholm.net; bus #50/53 from Central Station. A 10-minute walk from the station in a quiet residential area facing the leafy Tegnérlunden park, this small pension-style hotel has twelve en-suite rooms with beechwood furniture, modern Swedish decor and a pretty courtyard garden. KrKr

BLIQUE BY NOBIS MAP PAGE 36, POCKET MAP B2 Gävlegatan 18, Ⓦ bliquebynobis.se; St Eriksplan T-bana. Blique by Nobis is located in the up-and-coming arty district of Hagastaden – it's a little further out of town, but worth it.

This hotel is all about industrial chic, with raw concrete walls and floors; the room design is that classic Scandi combination of beauty and function, with neutral colour schemes. There are a variety of rooms on offer, including some without windows and some with kitchenettes. Blique has two sleek restaurants (one which specialises in Asian food and the other which combines Scandinavian seafood with classic Korean dishes) and two bars, one of which is on the rooftop and enjoys an incredible view. There's also a herb garden up here, from which bartenders pick fresh herbs for the cocktails, and there's even a cinema available for private screenings. KrKrKr

CITY BACKPACKERS MAP PAGE 36, POCKET MAP A10. Upplandsgatan 2A, Ⓦ citybackpackers.se; T-Centralen T-bana. A friendly, vibrant hostel with a hundred or so beds, a five-minute walk from Centralstationen. One for the youngsters or just the young at heart, skateboards are available for rent and there are regular movie nights and pub crawls. There are also free sauna sessions every night. Some rooms have private facilities. Kr

DOWNTOWN CAMPER BY SCANDIC MAP PAGE 36, POCKET MAP C11. Brunkebergstorg 9, Ⓦ scandichotels.com; T-Centralen T-bana. Downtown Camper is a distinguished hotel with a campfire and excellent barbecue and grill bar. It's located in a central position just behind Sergels Torg and the Kulturhuset, and has a fantastic pool and a great rooftop bar – but the showstopper here is really the buffet breakfast, which has a vast choice for all tastes and dietary requirements; there's an entire gluten-free and vegan section. KrKrKr

HOTEL C MAP PAGE 36, POCKET MAP B11. Vasaplan 4, Ⓦ hotelcstockholm.se; T-Centralen T-bana. This hotel is situated across the road from its sister hotel, Nordic Light. It has a rugged, close-to-nature atmosphere combined with all modern facilities. It is also home to the famous Ice Bar, made of pure ice and maintained at 5°C (23°F), where you can have a drink from a 'glass' made of ice. KrKrKr

HOTEL HELLSTEN MAP PAGE 36, POCKET MAP C3. Luntmakargatan 68, Ⓦ hellsten. se; Rådmansgatan T-bana. Located in a very trendy area, this is a hip hotel where each of the rooms – there are six different categories – has its own style, colour, textile design and furnishings. The junior suites are noted for their beautiful porcelain stoves and stuccoed ceilings. Seven of the rooms have balconies, and every Thursday the hotel's Earth Bar hosts premier jazz concerts. Overall, a great hotel with large rooms that represent excellent value for money. KrKrKr

MISS CLARA MAP PAGE 36, POCKET MAP D3. Sveavägen 48, Ⓦ missclarahotel.com; Hötorget T-bana. Housed in a stunning Art Nouveau building that was a girls' school until 1939 (the hotel is named after its most influential headmistress), Miss Clara is a marvellous choice. The hotel features spacious rooms with dark parquet floors, high ceilings, muted colour palettes and tall windows that let the light pour in, as well as incredibly comfortable beds, supremely soft linens, and the deepest bathtubs you've ever experienced. The staff are incredibly friendly and the buffet breakfast is top-notch, with a wide variety of options to choose from – all scrumptious. There's also a 24-hour sauna and a fantastic bar. Extremely highly recommended. KrKrKrKr

NOBIS MAP PAGE 36, POCKET MAP D10. Norrmalmstorg 2, Ⓦ nobishotel. se; Östermalmstorg T-bana. This posh, sophisticated hotel is housed in a pair of regal nineteenth-century buildings and enjoys a fantastic location, slap-bang in the middle of the shopping district and surrounded by restaurants, bars and nightclubs. It features wooden staircases and stone floors, and rooms mostly have courtyard, city or park views; some have whirlpool tubs. The opulent Gold Bar here is especially worth a visit – the name is literal, as the ceiling is plated with gold. KrKrKrKr

NORDIC LIGHT MAP PAGE 36, POCKET MAP B10. Vasaplan 7, Ⓦ nordiclighthotel. com; T-Centralen T-bana. Minimalist Nordic design reigns here; the hotel uses a unique lighting design which provides it with a truly Scandinavian feel. The standard rooms are individually decorated in shades of white and steely grey, inspired by Lapland's amazing northern lights. Contemporary rather than comfortable perhaps, but it's very near the train station. KrKrKrKr

QUEEN'S MAP PAGE 36, POCKET MAP B10. Drottninggatan 71A, Ⓦ queenshotel. se; Hötorget T-bana. Renovated with a mix of old and new, this central hotel offers individually decorated en-suite rooms that take their decorative cues from the turn of the last century. Surprisingly quiet, given the location in Stockholm's main shopping district. Very friendly staff. KrKrKr

SCANDIC GRAND CENTRAL MAP PAGE 36, POCKET MAP A10. Kungsgatan 70, Ⓦ scandichotels.com; T-Centralen T-bana. As the name suggests, this place is both grand and central, with a winning location near the train station. Standard rooms are modern and elegant; the 'cabins' are very compact. The stylish brasserie is a popular spot among locals seeking pre-theatre drinks. KrKrKr

SCANDIC NO 53 MAP PAGE 36, POCKET MAP B10. Kungsgatan 53, Ⓦ scandichotels. se/no53; Hötorget T-bana. This unfussy three-star hotel is a good option for those who want to stay centrally without breaking the bank. It's slick and modern with compact rooms, some of which are windowless. There's a sunlit patio for use in the summer and a handy shop at reception where you can buy food and bathroom essentials; meals are served in the colourful lounge on the ground floor. This hotel also has decent accessibility features; measurements are listed on the website, and there are wide hallways for wheelchairs. KrKr

HOTEL TEGNÉRLUNDEN MAP PAGE 36, POCKET MAP C3. Tegnérlunden 8, Ⓦ hoteltegnerlunden.se; Rådmansgatan T-bana. Located in a quiet square just off the pedestrian shopping street of Drottninggatan and a few minutes' walk from Central Station. Some of the rooms have lovely views over the park. Hotel Tegnérlunden is wheelchair-friendly and features a rooftop breakfast room and sauna. KrKrKr

Kungsholmen

CLARION HOTEL AMARANTEN MAP PAGE 46, POCKET MAP B4. Kungsholmsgatan 31, ⓦ nordicchoicehotels.com; Rådhuset T-bana. This is a large, modern hotel with bags of style that also features a spa, found in a neat area just a short walk from City Hall and Central Station. All rooms are clean and warmly decorated with flat-screen TVs; some have city views. Family rooms with baby equipment are also available, as are suites which have balconies and separate living rooms. KrKrKr

CONNECT CITY MAP PAGE 46, POCKET MAP A4. Ahlströmergatan 41, ⓦ connecthotels.se; Fridhemsplan T-bana. A bright, airy and modern hotel on Kungsholmen with oak floors, simple, colourful rooms, and fully tiled bathrooms. Some rooms don't have windows. It may be true that this hotel is never going to win any prizes for original design but at these prices it really doesn't matter. Kr

M/S MONIKA MAP PAGE 46, POCKET MAP A3. Kungsholms Strand 133, ⓦ msmonika. se; Fridhemsplan/St Eriksplan T-bana. One of Stockholm's more intimate 'floatels', this charming wooden boat from 1908 bobs around just off Kungsholmen's north shore. There are just three quirky but compact rooms, some of which have bunk beds or pull-out sofas; the whole boat can be rented out on request. There are sun loungers on the deck and a communal living room. KrKr

STOCKHOLM HOSTEL MAP PAGE 46, POCKET MAP A4. Ahlströmergatan 15, ⓦ stockholmhostel.se; Fridhemsplan T-bana. Bright, contemporary design hostel. Rooms all have private facilities and their own television – as beds aren't available to rent individually, you'll need to rent the whole room. Two large and well-equipped kitchens are available for guests' use. This is billed as a 'nicer' hostel experience, which means there are strict bans on parties and alcohol. Kr

Djurgården

BACKSTAGE HOTEL MAP PAGE 54, POCKET MAP F5. Djurgårdsvägen 68, ⓦ backstagehotelsthlm.com. A top choice of visiting popstars, the Backstage Hotel oozes effortless chic. There are varying sizes of room, but are all quirkily fitted out and quite retro. Its location is ideal for visiting the surrounding museums and galleries of Djurgården – it shares the same building as the ABBA: The Museum (see page 56) which is right next door, and guests of the hotel benefit from discounted entry. The staff are amazingly friendly and helpful, and rooms are surprisingly quiet, given that it's so close to Grona Lund. KrKrKr

HOTEL HASSELBACKEN MAP PAGE 54, POCKET MAP G5. Hazeliusbacken 20, ⓦ hasselbacken.com. Hotel Hasselbacken is perhaps most famous for its stunningly decorated, centuries-old restaurant (see page 60), which is the place where Hasselback potatoes were invented. The family- and pet-friendly hotel attached to the restaurant enjoys a handy location near to lots of museums and galleries. The rooms are simple and comfortable with marble bathrooms, and there's a sauna, gym, and bike rental available. KrKrKrKr

Blasieholmen & Skeppsholmen

AF CHAPMAN MAP PAGE 64, POCKET MAP D12. Flaggmansvägen 8, ⓦ booking.com/hotel/se/af-chapman; Kungsträdgården T-bana. This smart, square-rigged 1888 ship – a landmark in its own right – has views over Gamla Stan that are unsurpassed at the price and a real treat to wake up to. One of the quirkiest places to stay in Stockholm, though reservations are a must. Make sure you get a room aboard the boat, rather than on dry land. Kr

BERNS HOTEL MAP PAGE 64, POCKET MAP D11. Näckströmsgatan 8, ⓦ berns. se; Östermalmstorg T-bana. Hip, exclusive hotel with colourful and chic rooms of varying sizes – one has its own sauna, and some have whirlpool tubs. All rooms have distinguished contemporary decor designed around rich marble and cherry wood. There's a gym here, as well as various restaurants, a concert hall and a nightclub. Breakfast costs extra. KrKrKrKr

GRAND HÔTEL STOCKHOLM MAP PAGE 64, POCKET MAP D11. Södra Blaiseholmshamnen 8, Ⓦgrandhotel. se; Östermalmstorg T-bana.
Grand in size, architecture, style and graciousness, the Grand is the only hotel of its class in Sweden; unsurprisingly then, it is one of the most famous in Scandanavia. It has fantastic views across to the Royal Palace in Gamla Stan and Strömkajen, the departure point for Stockholm's numerous sightseeing boats, and there are gorgeous, up-market and very distinguished restaurants here (see page 69), as well as a Nordic spa. KrKrKrKr

HOTEL SKEPPSHOLMEN MAP PAGE 64, POCKET MAP E12. Gröna gången 1, Ⓦhotelskeppsholmen.se.
Set on the lush and peaceful island of Skeppsholmen and situated right by the water's edge, this stunning design hotel is housed in a government-listed yellow building that dates back to 1699; it originally served as the naval barracks for the Royal Marines, and later as a plague hospital. Today, LGBTQ+-run Hotel Skeppsholmen is eco-friendly and modern; parts of the building are made from materials that come ruins from around Sweden, adding to its colourful history. The rooms are light, airy, and boast stunning sea views, while the restaurant, Långa Raden (see page 68), is first rate. It's definitely worth sitting out on the patio to eat your meal if the sun is shining – and after lunch, you can play tennis on Sweden's first tennis court! KrKrKrKr

RADISSON COLLECTION STRAND HOTEL MAP PAGE 64, POCKET MAP D11. Nybrokajen 9, Ⓦradissonhotels. com; Östermalmstorg T-bana.
This hotel is set in a large, traditional, ivy-covered twentieth-century building overlooking the boats on Nybroviken Bay. Rooms are glossy, with sleek hardwood floors; some have water views and squashy armchairs and sofas, whilst business-class suites have separate sitting areas; a few even have fancy chandeliers, whilst others feature terraces. There's 24-hour room service and a sauna, plus a particularly posh lobby bar. KrKrKrKr

Södermalm

CLARION HOTEL STOCKHOLM MAP PAGE 72, POCKET MAP E8. Ringvägen 98, Ⓦstrawberryhotels.com; Skanstull T-bana.
This reasonably-priced hotel sits in a huge modern block with more than 500 rooms. Rates are decent compared with hotels in Gamla Stan, and there's parking right beneath the building. There's a gym, yoga classes, and lots of meeting rooms, making this popular with those travelling for business. KrKr

The Swedish sauna ritual

In Stockholm, most hotels and public swimming pools will have a sauna. They're generally electric and extra steam is created by tossing water onto the hot elements; the temperature inside ranges from 70°C to 120°C. Traditional wood-burning saunas are often found further out in the archipelago and give off a wonderful smell. Public saunas are usually single sex and nude, you'll often see signs forbidding the wearing of swimming costumes, as these would collect your sweat and allow it to soak into the wooden benches. It's common practice to take a cold shower afterwards or, in winter, roll in the snow to cool off; if you're in the archipelago, people often take a dip in the sea or lake – the feeling of euphoria that follows a cold-lake dip after a stint in the sauna is truly unbeatable, and supposedly comes with a host of health benefits. Common wisdom states that ten minutes in the sauna should be followed by two minutes in the cold water, repeated three or four times.

HELLSTENS GLASHUS MAP PAGE 72, POCKET MAP D7. Wollmar Yxkullsgatan 13, Ⓦ hellstensglashus.se; Mariatorget T-bana. Hip and cool, Hellstens Glashus finds itself situated in the heart of the most interesting, trendy and popular area of Stockholm. The rooms are smartly fitted out with colourful accents; some boast spectacular floor-to-ceiling windows. The lobby of the hotel looks out onto a street buzzing with cafés and bars through a unique, 7-metre glass façade that can be opened up in summer. Down here, you'll also find a restaurant and bar whose floor showcases exposed bedrock that is hundreds of thousands of years old. KrKrKr

LÅNGHOLMENS HOTELL MAP PAGE 72, POCKET MAP A6. Långholmsmuren 20, Ⓦ langholmen.com. On the island of Långholmen, this place was built as a prison in the early nineteenth century, but closed in 1975. It was then converted to an unusual hotel and hostel fourteen years later. It's a fun place to stay, and full of history, with big bathrooms and a good breakfast. It's also in an incredibly breath-taking location for a prison, with waterfront views and lots of lush greenery. Expect small rooms – or rather, cells – but surprisingly comfy beds. KrKr

DEN RÖDA BÅTEN MAP PAGE 72, POCKET MAP D6. Södermälarstrand Kajplats 10, Ⓦ theredboat.com; Slussen T-bana. Den Röda Båten means The Red Boat; this makes sense, as this unfussy hostel is housed in an old Göta canal steamer and an adjacent boat. It enjoys a fantastic location overlooking the city hall, and the cabins, which sleep up to four people in bunk beds, are compact but comfortable and clean. There are no cooking facilities on board due to the risk of fire. Kr

RIVAL MAP PAGE 72, POCKET MAP D6. Mariatorget 3, Ⓦ rival.se; Mariatorget T-bana. Widley hailed as Stockholm's first boutique hotel, Rival is owned by Benny Andersson of ABBA who designed the hotel in a combination of 1930s and contemporary Swedish style to recapture the former glamour of the building. The rooms are warmly and colourfully decorated, with enlarged stills from classic Swedish films hanging above the beds. Some rooms have balconies overlooking the square, and the building includes a bistro, a bakery, and even a cinema. The hotel also has excellent accessibility features which are listed on its website. KrKrKrKr

SCANDIC MALMEN MAP PAGE 72, POCKET MAP E7. Götgatan 49–51, Ⓦ scandichotels.com/malmen; Medborgarplatsen T-bana. Comfortable, if predictable, chain hotel rooms with wooden floors and modern Scandinavian decor. The quality of the rooms vary massively – some are small and windowless, but some of the more expensive rooms have freestanding bathtubs and multiple bedrooms. It's the location that really makes this massive hotel worth considering – it's super close to the trendy district of SoFo. KrKrKr

SKANSTULL'S HOSTEL MAP PAGE 72, POCKET MAP E8. Ringvägen 135, Ⓦ skanstulls.se; Skanstull T-bana. Bright, quirky rooms and mixed dorms at this excellent, laid-back hostel near SoFo's bars and restaurants in Södermalm. There's a stylish kitchen and dining area complete with free tea, coffee and pasta. Linens and towels are available to rent at a small extra cost. Kr

TRE SMÅ RUM MAP PAGE 72, POCKET MAP D7. Högbergsgatan 81, Ⓦ tresmarum. se; Mariatorget T-bana. A clean, comfy option in the heart of Södermalm that gives real value for money; the seven simple basement rooms with shared bathrooms are very popular, so book in advance. A stay feels more like stopping off at a friend's than staying in a hotel; there's even a help-yourself breakfast available from the kitchen fridge, often with delicious home-made bread. Kr

ZINKENSDAMM MAP PAGE 72, POCKET MAP C7. Zinkens Väg 20, Ⓦ zinkensdamm. com; Zinkensdamm T-bana. There is a hostel and a hotel in this building; the hotel is made up of comfortable, well-appointed and homely hotel rooms, all en-suite, with tasteful wallpaper and wooden floors. The hostel itself is huge, with private rooms and single-sex dorms, with kitchen and laundry facilities also available. It's in a good location for exploring Södermalm, right on the doorstep of Tantolunden park – though it's a 30-minute walk from the city centre. KrKr

Östermalm

HOTEL DIPLOMAT MAP PAGE 84, POCKET MAP D10. Strandvägen 7, Ⓦ diplomathotel. com; Östermalmstorg T-bana. A delightful Jugend-style building dating from 1911 with a fine waterfront location. Family-owned, this Art Nouveau townhouse offers individually designed rooms with elegant furnishings, lovely high ceilings and wonderful views over Stockholm's inner harbour. A really beautiful place to stay in a fantastic location. KrKrKrKr

HOTEL ESPLANADE MAP PAGE 84, POCKET MAP D10. Strandvägen 7A, Ⓦ hotelesplanade.se; Östermalmstorg T-bana. Behind an attractive Jugend façade, there is a small, charming, family-owned hotel. All rooms have been individually decorated to a high standard. Excellent location close to the Royal Palace and Opera House, with views over Nybroviken Bay. KrKrKr

HOTEL KUNG CARL MAP PAGE 84, POCKET MAP D4. Birger Jarlsgatan 21, Ⓦ hkchotels.se; Östermalmstorg T-bana. Family-run Kung Carl claims to be the oldest in Stockholm; it celebrated its 155th anniversary in 2022. Greta Garbo is known to have stayed here several times, as has Selma Lagerlöf, the first woman to be awarded the Nobel Prize for Literature – it's rumoured that she finished one of her novels in one of Kung Carl's rooms. This beautiful hotel is also one of the most centrally located hotels in Stockholm; it's situated right on Stureplan, an area known for its designer shops, restaurants, bars and nightclubs. Each room is individually designed, and they vary from the traditional to the trendy – go for the ice cream room if you have a sweet tooth! There's a fantastic French bistro here, as well as two bars and a jazz club that hosts live jazz as well as DJs, stand-up comedy on Thursdays, and drag bingo on Wednesdays. KrKrKr

VILLA DAGMAR MAP PAGE 84, POCKET MAP D10. Nybrogatan 25, Ⓦ hotelvilladagmar.com; Östermalmstorg T-bana. Villa Dagmar is a refined hotel on a quiet, pedestrianised street, close to various shops, bars and eateries. It was inspired by an Italian villa in Capri, which explains its Mediterranean restaurant and distinctly southern-European feel – it's bright and airy, with yellow walls. The hotel itself is based in three buildings, a former apartment block and an old sweet factory as well as a smart new redbrick; the three are connected by a leafy, covered courtyard, and the rooms are small but quirky; some have designer wallpaper, and all have marble bathrooms. There's a buzzy bar that hosts live music or DJs most nights, as well as 24-hour room service and sound healing workshops (!) on Thursdays. KrKrKr

Day trips

ÄNGBY CAMPING Blackebergsvägen 20, Ⓦ angbycamping.se; Ängbyplan T-bana. A clean, comfortable and friendly campsite with shower and toilet facilities. Offers small wooden cabins with stoves and fridges, as well as tent pitches. It's not luxurious, but it has everything you need, and enjoys a pretty idyllic location; it's situated west of the city on the lakeshore where there are good beaches, but is still only around 5 minutes from the nearest T-bana. It's open all year round, but it's best to phone ahead to book between September and April when it can get busy. Kr

BREDÄNG CAMPING Stora Sällskapets Väg, Ⓦ bredangcamping.se; Bredäng T-bana. Southwest of the city with views over Lake Mälaren and lots of good swimming spots. The site has good access to the city centre – it takes about 30 minutes to get to Gamla Stan on the T-bana. Generally clean with friendly staff. Open all year, though only the campsite's cabins are open between mid-Oct and mid-April. Kr

CLARION HOTEL GILLET Dragarbrunnsgatan 23, Uppsala, Ⓦ clarionhotelgillet.se. A perfect location in the centre of Uppsala, within walking distance of all of the city's main attractions. Understated but clean and comfortable rooms with colourful accents; there's also 24-hour room service as well as a pool, gym, sauna and an excellent restaurant serving American-influenced dishes. Finally, there's a trendy bar with great views over Uppsala. KrKrKr

SANDHAMNS VÄRDSHUS Main village, Sandhamn, ⓦsandhamns-vardshus.se. An agreeable bed-and-breakfast establishment housed in an attractive timber building by the shore in Sandhamn, also serving excellent seafood. It pays to book in advance as there are only half a dozen rooms available – all sharing facilities. KrKr

SEGLARHOTELLET Main village, Sandhamn, ⓦsandhamn.com. An exclusive and rather swanky hotel in Sandhamn, catering for wealthy yachties and serving excellent seafood; some of the rooms have desirable balconies overlooking the sea.

Self-catering apartments also available. KrKrKrKr

SMÅDALARÖ GÅRD Smådalarövägen 100, Dalarö, ⓦsmadalarogard.se. One of Sweden's largest and most chic countryside spa hotels, Smådalarö Gård is manages to maintain a laidback atmosphere even as it is set in a stunning nineteenth-century mansion on the waterfront. Some rooms have four-poster beds and suites have separate living room areas; the rooms with terraces and harbour views are particularly lovely. The hotel offers curative experiences including a stunning spa area, locally sourced dining at the gorgeous terrace restaurant and an outdoor pub with regular live music. Perhaps the best part is the traditional Swedish wood-fired saunas, from which you can jump directly into the Baltic for a quick dose of wholesome euphoria. KrKrKrKr

ACCOMMODATION

ESSENTIALS

T-bana metro train

Arrival

By plane

There are direct flights to Stockholm from many destinations, including the UK, France, Germany, Greece, Portugal and Spain. There are currently no direct flights to Stockholm operating from Australia or South Africa.

Most flights to Stockholm arrive at Arlanda airport (ⓦ arlanda.se/en), 45km north of Stockholm. The fastest way to get between Stockholm's Centralstationen (Central Station) and Arlanda airport is on the carbon neutral Arlanda Express train (ⓦ arlandaexpress.com), which runs entirely on electricity from renewable energy sources. The journey takes 18 minutes and services run frequently (at least every 15 minutes) between 5am and midnight. The main company operating buses into Stockholm is Flygbussarna (ⓦ flygbussarna.se); all-day services run to Stockholm's long-distance bus station, Cityterminalen, every 10–15min.

Some domestic flights arrive at the more central Bromma airport, which handles more than 1 million people every year to and from other parts of Scandinavia. Bromma is connected to Cityterminalen by Flygbussarna; buses run two to three times per hour and take 20 minutes.

Most of Ryanair's Stockholm flights arrive at Skavsta airport, 100km south of the capital close to the town of Nyköping; others come in to Västerås, 100km west of Stockholm. Skavsta and Västerås buses operate in connection with flight arrival and departure times.

By train

Stockholm is easily accessible by rail from Copenhagen, Denmark and Oslo, Norway. You'll arrive at Stockholm Centralstationen (the station is also known as Stockholm C, which is an abbreviation of 'Central' in railspeak throughout Sweden), a cavernous structure on Vasagatan in the city centre. All branches of the tunnelbana (or T-bana), Stockholm's efficient metro system, meet at T-Centralen, which is the T-bana station directly below the main station. Interrail offers the One Country Pass train travel within Sweden on three, four, five, six or eight days within a one-month period (ⓦ interrail.eu/en/interrail-passes/one-country-pass/sweden). Eurail (ⓦ eurail.com) offers a similar pass for those not living in Europe, as well as a Scandinavia Pass, which covers Sweden, Denmark, Norway and Finland. There are discounts for travellers under the age of 28. A high-speed train runs between Stockholm Central Station and Malmö Centralstation, in southern Sweden (4hr 10min). From here, it's an easy bus ride (40min) to Copenhagen.

By bus

By bus, your arrival point will be the huge glass structure known as Cityterminalen, a high-tech terminal adjacent to Centralstationen which handles all bus services. You can get to the northern end of Centralstationen's main hall using a series of escalators and walkways.

By car

Taxis from the airport into town (30–40min) can be expensive. Fares are typically around €47 - make sure you agree on a price before you set off. If you are driving yourself into central Stockholm, be aware that you will be subject to a congestion charge; cameras register vehicles automatically and your credit card will be debited accordingly

Getting around

Stockholm is, generally speaking, a very walkable and picturesque city. However, there are various reliable, clean and eco-friendly public transport systems that you may wish to make use of during your visit.

Public transport

Storstockholms Lokaltrafik (SL; ⓦsl. se) operates a comprehensive system of buses and underground trains, which extends well out of the city centre. Up-to-date information on the public transport system in English can be found on their website. One option is to buy a travelcard, available from Pressbyrån newsagents, SL-Centers and the ticket machines at T-bana stations: first, buy SL's Access card, a smartcard onto which you load the travelcard you want; you are then entitled to unlimited travel by bus and T-bana. You can also tap into the T-bana with your bank card. Note that you can't purchase tickets with cash on the city's buses; it's travelcard or bank card only.

T-bana

The quickest and most useful form of transport is the Tunnelbana (T-bana; ⓦsl.se), Stockholm's metro system, which comprises three main lines (red, green and blue). Station entrances are marked with a blue letter 'T' on a white background. From Sunday to Thursday trains operate from around 5am until around midnight, but on Fridays and Saturdays – as well as the evening before a public holiday – there are services all through the night (roughly every 30–40min).

Buses

Stockholm's buses are often less direct than the metro because of the city's layout; bus #4 is an excellent way of seeing a lot of the city for very little cost. You can't buy tickets from the driver; get a travelcard instead, or tap on with your bank card. Buses are pushchair- and wheelchair-friendly; a special area halfway down the bus is set aside for these. Night buses replace the T-bana after midnight, except days when the T-bana runs all night (see page 117).

Ferries and boats

Ferries link some of the central islands: Djurgården is connected with Slussen (at the southern end of Gamla Stan) and Skeppsholmen, with services roughly every 20 minutes. Ferries also provide frequent, year-round access to the sprawling archipelago, and sail from outside the Grand hotel on Strömkajen near the Nationalmuseum. Ferries can be lovely activities in and of themselves and allow lovely views of the islands that make up the city.

By bike and scooter

You can rent bikes from Servicedepån Gardefuhr at Scheelegatan 15 on Kungsholmen (ⓦcykelstallet.se). There are also now various e-scooter hire apps through which you can rent a scooter; try Voi, Lime and Tier.

By taxis

Taxis in Stockholm are very safe, but their prices are unregulated, meaning that journey costs can vary significantly depending on which taxi you get into. While you may be paying the fare to a licensed driver by meter, individual drivers are allowed by law to set their own prices and the cost of a journey can vary significantly from car to car; in some cases, they can be eye-wateringly expensive. Your best bet is to use either the ubiquitous Taxi Stockholm (☏08 15 00 00,

Ⓦ taxistockholm.se) or Taxi Kurir (Ⓣ 30 00 00, Ⓦ taxikurir.se) which have the most reasonable, fixed prices that all their drivers adhere to; their vehicles are almost always 'green' or electric/hybrid cards. Both also have mobile apps that will allow you to pay via your credit card online. Remember to look carefully at the taxi livery, as many private taxi firms have similar designs to these companies. Uber and other rideshare apps are also widely available.

By car

In reality, visitors to Stockholm will find that having a car is more of a hindrance than a help. The public transport system is superb and the numerous boats that ply the waters of the archipelago are an attraction in their own right. Besides that, car hire and petrol are expensive, and the penalties for speeding and other restrictions are severe. There is also a congestion charge for entering the city centre. However, if you are planning a tour around Sweden, then hiring a car before you go can help you to avoid any uncertainties. Some car hire companies to try are Avis, Europcar, Budget and Hertz, all with offices at Arlanda Airport. If you decide to hire once you are in Stockholm, then you can contact Avis on Ⓣ 010-49 48 050; Europcar on Ⓣ 08-21 06 50; Budget on Ⓣ 8503 83 333; or Hertz on Ⓣ 08 454-62 50.

Directory A–Z

Accessible travel

Sweden is, in many ways, a model of awareness in terms of accessible travel; accessibility is a governmental policy priority, and assistance is forthcoming from virtually all Swedes if needed. Sweden's capital city, then, is one of the easiest cities to visit for those with access needs, in part due to a 1998 city council initiative that aimed to make Stockholm the world's most accessible capital city.

In terms of public transport, almost every T-bana station is accessible by lift, and trains and platforms are nearly always at the same level. Buses are equipped for wheelchairs and staff are trained and always willing to assist where necessary. The transport system provides in-depth and up-to-date accessibility information on its website at Ⓦ sl.se/en/eng-info/getting-around/accessibility. As for getting around, there are extensive dropped kerbs and pedestrian crossings; one place that wheelchair users may find difficult is Gamla Stan, where the streets are narrow and cobblestoned. Accommodation suitable for people with access needs is readily available. Any building with three or more storeys must, by law, have a lift installed, while all public buildings are legally required to be accessible to people with disabilities and have automatic doors. To check the accessibility of restaurants, check the comprehensive online database Tillgänglighetsdatabasen (Ⓦ t-d.se/en). Almost all museums, galleries and sights in Stockholm have excellent accessibility provisions.

For more information, the De Handikappades Riksförbund website is very useful (Ⓦ dhr.se), as is the information available on the Visit Sweden website (Ⓦ visitsweden.com/about-sweden/accessible-travel).

Addresses

Swedish addresses begin with the street name and building number. In Sweden, as in many European countries, it is common to place the street name before the building number. This is followed by the post code; the Swedish postcode system is based on a five-digit number combination, divided into two groups of three and two digits. Stockholm postcodes begin with number 1. A typical Stockholm address would look like this:

Djurgårdsvägen 68 (street name, building number)

115 21 Stockholm (post code, geographical location)

Children

Sweden is an exemplary country when it comes to travelling with children. Most hotels and youth hostels have family rooms and both men's and women's toilets – including those on trains – usually offer baby-changing areas. Stockholm in particular is a city with a host of child-friendly attractions and activities on offer; it's always a good idea to ask for children's discounts, as many activities, particularly during the summer months, are geared towards families. One major children's attraction is the archipelago's countless islets, which provide ample opportunity for boating, swimming and fishing. Other highlights that will please children (and kids of all ages) include Gröna Lund, a summer-only amusement park full of rides and other activities (see page 56) and Skansen, a brilliant open-air museum that is perfect for families, with a mix of animals (including petting zoo, aquarium and even a crocodile pond), historical buildings and cafés (see page 57).

Cinema

Cinema-going is an incredibly popular pastime in Stockholm. There are a good number of cinemas the entire length of Kungsgatan between Sveavägen and Birger Jarlsgatan, which are always very lively on Saturday night. Foreign films are always shown in the original language with Swedish subtitles, and never dubbed. The largest cinema in the city centre is Filmstaden Sergel, located at Hötorget 8 (sf.se).

Crime and emergencies

Sweden is one of the safest countries in the world. Nevertheless, it is good sense not to leave bags unattended and to keep an eye on your valuables when you're out and about, particularly in Gamla Stan where pickpockets are known to take advantage of distracted tourists in the narrow and crowded streets. Keep tabs on your cash and passport and you should have little reason to visit the police station; if you do, you're likely to find them courteous, concerned and usually able to speak brilliant English.

The emergency number in Sweden is 112. This covers the ambulance (*ambulans*), rescue service, fire department (*brandkår*), police (*polis*), as well as air/sea and mountain rescue services, the poison hot line and on-call doctors. It can be dialled free of charge (no coins needed) from any telephone. English is usually understood.

Discount passes

The Stockholm Pass, also known as the Go City All-Inclusive Pass, offers you the chance to save money on some of Stockholm's main attractions. It offers the holder free entry to over 60 museums, castles and other attractions (including, but by no means limited to, the Vasa Museum, the Viking Museum, Skansen and Artipelag) as well as some bus and boat tours. The pass is available as an app, but can also be printed out for those worries about battery life. They vary in price depending on which card you opt for – they are valid for between one and five days – and when used to the full, the card represents a considerable bargain. You can buy a pass online at ⓦ gocity.com/stockholm.

Electricity

The supply for electric appliances in Sweden is 220 volt, 50 Hz AC, and requires standard two-pin, round continental plugs.

Embassies & consulates

Embassies, with consulate sections, are generally open Monday to Friday 8.30am–4.30pm, but there is usually a 24-hour telephone service in operation.

Australia: Klarabergsviadukten 63, 8th Floor, 101 36 Stockholm, ☎ 08-613 2900, ⓦ sweden.embassy.gov.au.

Republic of Ireland: Hovslagargatan 5, 111 48 Stockholm, ☎ 08-5450 4040, ⓦ embassyofireland.se.

New Zealand: Skarpögatan 6, 115 27 Stockholm, ☎ 08-400 17 270, ⓦ mfat. govt.nz/en/countries-and-regions/ europe/sweden/new-zealand-embassy.

South Africa: Alsnögatan 7, 6th Floor, 116 44 Stockholm, ☎ 08-2439 50, ⓦ gov. za/about-government/contact-directory/ representatives-rsa/representatives-rsa/sweden-kingdom-south.

UK: Skarpögatan 6-8, 115 93 Stockholm, ☎ 08-671 30 00, ⓦ gov.uk/ world/sweden.

US: Dag Hammarskjölds Väg 31, 115 89 Stockholm, ☎ 08 783 53 00; ⓦ usemb.se.

Health

No vaccinations are needed for entry to Sweden.

EU residents should obtain the European Health Insurance Card, which entitles them to emergency medical and hospital treatment; note that this has changed to the Global Health Insurance Card for UK citizens (ⓦ services.nhsbsa.nhs.uk/cra). Citizens of non-EU countries should ensure they have adequate travel/ health insurance before leaving home.

If you fall ill, have an accident or are in need of a doctor, call the 24-hour healthcare information line on ☎ 1177 for advice and information about where to find your nearest healthcare centre (see also ⓦ 1177. se/en/Stockholm/other-languages/ other-languages). You could also ask someone such as your hotel receptionist to call a doctor on your behalf; make sure the doctor is affiliated with Försäkringskassan (Swedish National Health Service).

In an emergency, call 112 for an ambulance; if you are able, go to a hospital's emergency and casualty reception (*akutmottagning*); take your passport with you for identification. Any prescriptions need to be taken to a chemist (*apoteket*).

Chemists/pharmacies stock over-the-counter products like cough medicine and aspirin and also supply prescriptions. A 24-hour pharmacy service is offered by C.W. Scheele at Klarabergsgatan 64 near the Centralstationen (ⓦ apoteket. se/apotek/apoteket-c-w-scheele-stockholm). You can also call them on ☎ 0771-450 450, which is the number for general pharmacy information throughout Sweden. Nevertheless, it is a good idea to bring along an adequate supply of any prescribed medication from home.

Tap water and ice are perfectly safe to drink throughout Sweden.

Internet

Almost all accommodation establishments and most restaurants and cafés offer free internet access to guests. Elsewhere, you can get online for free at Pressbyrån newsagents.

Left luggage

There are left luggage lockers (*förvaringsboxar*) of two different sizes available at Stockholm's Central Station. The lockers are located on the lower floor in the Stockholm City part of the station where the commuter trains arrive. Lockers can be rented for 4 hours at a time, or for a whole day.

LGBTQ+ travellers

Sweden is one of the world's most progressive countries when it comes to rights for LGBTQ+ people. Since 1988 government legislation has granted same-sex relationships the same status as heterosexual marriages and the state has given financial support to gay organisations; you are very likely to see rainbow flags hung from restaurants, cafés and other outlets wherever you go. Stockholm plays host to Scandinavia's largest pride parade each year in August, with 50,000 people marching in the parade and 500,000 more lining the streets – in a city with a population of just under one million, that's quite something! QX (Ⓦ qx. se) is a queer magazine that offers information about clubs, restaurants, bars and shops; you may see their 'Queermap' dotted around town which highlights some of the best spots. You can also find this map on their website. Some fantastic queer nightlife events to look up include Milq (men, Ⓦ instagram.com/ milqstockholm), Tuck o Hej (mixed, Ⓦ instagram.com/tuckohej), Clean Group Events (mixed, Ⓦ facebook. com/CleanGroup) and Moxy (women, Ⓦ instagram.com/moxystockholm).

Lost property

If you lose something in Stockholm, retracing your steps and asking at the most recent places you have visited is likely to yield results. If not, there is a lost and found service run by the police; you can find out more information (as well as reporting an item you have found) online at Ⓦ lost-found.org/stockholm-city.

Money

The Swedish currency is the krona (kr; plural kronor). It comes in coins of 1kr, 5kr and 10kr, and notes of 20kr, 50kr, 100kr, 200kr, 500kr and 1000kr. Confusingly, Sweden, Denmark and Norway all use the kronor as their national currency, and to distinguish between them they are abbreviated as SEK, DKK and NOK, respectively.

Stockholm is well on its way to becoming a completely cashless city; you can use your card to pay for goods and services almost everywhere, including taxis. Card readers are even commonplace even in smaller shops and markets, and Mastercard, Visa, American Express and Diners Card are widely accepted. You can also use your bank card to tap into or onto all public transport.

However, should you want to access cash whilst in Stockholm, the cheapest and easiest way of to do so is from ATMs with your debit card. There will be a flat transaction fee for withdrawals, which is usually quite small. Banks have standard exchange rates, but commissions can vary enormously. The best place to change money is at the yellow Forex offices (Ⓦ forex.se), which tend to offer more kronor for your currency though also charge commission.

VAT or sales tax is called Moms in Sweden (Ⓦ meridianglobalservices. com/country-profile-sweden) and is 25 percent on most goods and services (12 percent for accommodation). Up to 19 percent refund is available to non-EU residents on products valued at more than 200kr. Moms will be refunded in cash at any point of departure to visitors who have made purchases in shops displaying the blue-and-yellow 'Tax-Free Shopping' sticker. You should present your

Eating price codes

Throughout the Guide, we have categorised restaurant and café prices using a range of price codes (Kr being the symbol for Swedish krona). The categories below are based on a two-course meal with a soft drink, per person.

Kr = below 300kr
KrKr = 300–500kr
KrKrKr = 500–1,000kr
KrKrKrKr = over 1,000kr

passport at the time of purchase. Later, simply hand over the tax-free shopping receipt provided by the shop (be sure to fill in the back), at the tax-free service counter in ports, airports and aboard ships. This refund is available only for a limited period after purchase and is only open to those who are not EU residents.

Opening hours

Shops and department stores in Stockholm are usually open on weekdays 10am–6.30pm and on Saturdays until 4pm. Department stores tend to stay open later and are often open on Sunday afternoons. Food shops also have longer hours and are open on Sunday afternoons. Certain food shops, närbutiker, are open every day of the year from either 7am–11pm, or 10am–10pm. Banks are generally open Mon–Fri 10am–3pm (until 6pm on Thu), but are closed at weekends and on public holidays. Museums are usually open Tue–Sun 10 or 11am to 5–6pm. Chemists are generally open during normal shopping hours; a number stay open on duty at night and on Sundays.

Phones

The country code for Sweden is 46. The city code for Stockholm is 08; the initial 0, though, is dropped when making an international call to Sweden. The 08 is dropped when calling within Stockholm, unless dialling from a mobile phone. Any number beginning with 020 indicates a toll-free call.

The last public phone boots were dismantled in 2015 as mobile phones became more ubiquitous.

Charges for mobile phone roaming may be high for travellers outside of the EU, which now includes travellers from the UK; remember to check before you leave and turn off mobile data to avoid a nasty shock when you receive your bill. For longer stays and cheaper rates, a local SIM card is the best option. Various outlets supply these, but a major centre is Elgiganten Phonehouse (Sveavägen 26). You can also order a Swedish sim card from the Lycamobile website (ⓦlycamobile.se).

Post offices

The main post office is at Centralstationen (ⓦposten.se). Many grocery stores and corner shops also offer postal services; check 7-Eleven and Pressbyrån. To receive your mail general delivery (poste restante) have it sent to the Central Post Office, Stockholm 11120. Post boxes can be found in the street – blue for local mail, yellow for non-local.

Smoking

You can buy cigarettes in Sweden from the age of 18, though on the whole, Swedes tend not to be smokers; in 2021, it was reported that only 6% of the population smoked daily. Smoking is banned in all of Sweden's restaurants, bars, cafés and nightclubs, and since 2019 the ban also applies to these outlets' outdoor seating areas. Smoking is also prohibited at bus stops, on train platforms, in playgrounds and outside the entrances of hospitals and other public buildings.

Perhaps one reason for this is the growing prevalence of an oral tobacco product called 'snus', which often comes in sachets that look like tiny teabags and is placed between upper lip and gum for extended periods of time. The of this product is currently illegal in the UK and all EU-countries except Sweden.

Time

Sweden conforms to Central European Time (CET), which is always one hour ahead of Britain and Ireland. For most of the year Sweden is six hours ahead of New York, nine hours behind Sydney and eleven hours behind Auckland. Clocks go forward by one hour in late March and back one hour in late October (on the same days as in Britain and Ireland).

Tipping

Gratuities in Sweden are welcomed but not always expected, and service charges are often automatically added to hotel and restaurant bills at a rate of around 10 or 15 per cent. It is usual (but optional) to round up a restaurant bill to the nearest sensible denomination; for example, 277kr becomes 300kr, but there is no tradition of routinely tipping by ten to fifteen percent as in some countries.

Toilets

Public facilities are located in some underground stations, department stores and some of the bigger streets, squares and parks. They are often labelled with symbols for men and women, or marked WC, Damer/Herrar (Ladies/Gentlemen) or simply D/H. You are likely to find baby-changing facilities in both the men's and women's toilets. Public toilets are rarely free of charge, unless in a restaurant or café; some have slots for coins or an attendant to give towels and soap. The usual charge is 5kr.

Tourist information

The Stockholm Visitor Centre at Kulturhuset (Sergels Torg 3–5; ⓦ visitstockholm.com) is the main tourist office in Stockholm and offers maps, books and other tourist information. You can buy tickets here for excursions, sightseeing and concerts, Stockholm Passes and use free Wi-Fi. The Swedish Travel and Tourism Council also has a useful website for tourists at ⓦ visitsweden.com.

Festival and events

The Swedes may be modern in their social and sexual attitudes, but they are very traditional when it comes to celebrations, and festivals brighten the Swedish calendar throughout the year.

Walpurgis Night

30 April
Valborg or Walpurgis Night has its roots in Viking times. Huge bonfires blaze across the country, saluting the arrival of spring; in Stockholm, students hold torchlight parades and toast spring in verse, speeches and songs.

May Day

1 May
A statutory holiday. Political marches are usually held on this day.

Archipelago Boat Day

First Wednesday in June
Numerous steamboats make their way over to Vaxholm Island.

Swedish National Day

6 June
The Swedish National Day is celebrated with flags and parades. There is a ceremony when the king and Royal Family present flags to honour organisations and individuals.

Midsummer Eve

Friday between 20 June and 26 June
On the longest day of the year (Midsummer Eve), colourful maypoles decorated with garlands of birch boughs and wildflowers are raised in village and town squares all over Sweden. Dancing, along with a fair amount of drinking and merrymaking, continues far into the night, which in midsummer is as bright as day. In Stockholm, anyone can join the Midsummer Eve festivities at Skansen (see page 57).

Stockholm Pride

First week of August
The first week of August is given over to Stockholm Pride (ⓦ stockholmpride. org), a weeklong calendar of events, talks and celebrations, culminating in Scandinavia's largest Pride Parade on the Saturday.

Kräftskiva

August
The kräftskiva, or crayfish party (see page 61), is a highlight on the Swedish calendar, involving lots of food, drinking, singing and – obviously – crayfish. Traditionally, crayfish season began on the first Wednesday of August, although nowadays there is no set date.

Lidingöloppet

September
Lidingöloppet (ⓦ lidingoloppet.se), the world's largest cross-country race, is held at Lidingö.

Nobel Prize Day

10 December
A week of cultural and scientific events culminates in Nobel Prize Day when the prestigious prizes are given at a ceremony in the Stockholm Concert Hall.

St Lucia Day

13 December
Young girls dressed in long white gowns are crowned with wreaths of lighted candles that symbolise light breaking through the winter darkness. They sing a special song and serve saffron buns, *glögg* (mulled wine) and coffee.

Chronology

c.1252 Stockholm founded, probably by Birger Jarl

1397 Kalmar Union links the Nordic countries.

1520 Swedish noblemen executed in the 'Stockholm Bloodbath'.

1523 Gustav Vasa crowned king of Sweden after defeating the Danes.

1611 Gustav II Adolf comes to power.

1618 The Thirty Years' War starts in Germany.

1644 Gustav's daughter Kristina crowned

1654 Kristina abdicates, converts to Catholicism and moves to Rome.

1697 Tre Kronor Castle destroyed by fire; Karl XII, aged 15, is crowned.

1719 Constitution transfers power from the king to parliament.

1772 King Gustav III reclaims absolute power.

1786 Swedish Academy founded.

1809 Sweden loses Finland; Gustav IV Adolf abdicates.

1814 Sweden gains Norway in peace with Denmark.

1818 Karl XIV Johan crowned king of Sweden and Norway.

1876 L.M. Eriksson starts the manufacture of telephones.

1895 Alfred Nobel establishes the Nobel Prize.

1905 Parliament dissolves the union with Norway.

1939 Sweden's coalition government declares neutrality in World War II.

1950 Stockholm's first underground railway is inaugurated.

1955 Obligatory national health insurance established.

1974 The monarch loses all political powers. ABBA win the Eurovision Song Contest with 'Waterloo'.

1986 Prime Minister Olof Palme is murdered in Stockholm.

1995 Sweden joins the European Union after a referendum.

2000 Church separates from the state after four hundred years.

2003 Foreign Minister Anna Lindh murdered in Stockholm.

2006 Centre-right alliance headed by the Moderate Party wins election.

2010 The Sweden Democrats gain parliamentary seats for the first time.

2014 Social Democrats return to power in coalition with the Greens; the Sweden Democrats gain influence with 49 deputies.

2017 Five people are killed in a terrorist attack when a truck is driven into a crowd on Drottninggatan.

2023 Sweden wins the Eurovision Song Contest with Loreen's performance of her song 'Tattoo'; Sweden now has seven Eurovision wins, meaning it is tied with Ireland for the highest number of victories. Sweden also celebrates the 500-year anniversary of the Vasa crown and the fiftieth jubilee of the current King, Carl XVI Gustaf.

Language

For most foreigners, Swedish is an obscure language spoken by a few million people on the fringe of Europe. There is no need whatsoever to speak Swedish to enjoy a visit to Sweden – recent surveys have shown that an impressive 95 percent of Swedes speak English to some degree. However, Swedish deserves closer inspection, and if you master even a couple of phrases, you'll be met with nothing but words of encouragement. Check out our list of basic phrases to get started.

Basic phrases

yes/no ja/nej
hello hej/tjänare
good morning god morgon
good afternoon god middag
good night god natt
today/tomorrow idag/imorgon
please tack/var så god
here you are/you're welcome var så god
thank you (very much) tack (så mycket)
where?/when? var?/när/hur dags?
what?/why? vad?/varför?
how (much)? hur (mycket)?
I don't know jag vet inte

do you know? (a fact) vet du...?
could you...? skulle du kunna...?
sorry/excuse me förlåt/ursäkta
here/there här/där
near/far nära/avlägsen
this/that det här/det där
now/later nu/senare
more/less mera/mindre
big/little stor/liten
open/closed öppet/stängt
women/men kvinnor/män
toilet toalett
bank/change bank/växel
where are you from? varifrån kommer du?
I'm English jag är engelsman/engelska
...Scottish ...skotte
...Welsh ...walesare
...Irish ...irländare
...American ...amerikan
...Canadian ...kanadensare
...Australian ...australier
...a New Zealander ...nyzeeländare
what's your name? vad heter du?
what's this called in Swedish? vad heter
det här på svenska?
do you speak English? talar du engelska?
I don't understand jag förstår inte
how much is it? hur mycket kostar det?
skål cheers!

Getting around

how do I get to...? hur kommer jag till...?
left/right till vänster/till höger
straight ahead rakt fram
where is the bus station? var ligger
busstationen?
the bus stop for... busshållplatsen till...
train station järnvägsstationen/centralen
where does the bus to... leave from?
varifrån går bussen till...?
what time does it leave? hur dags går
det?
I'm going to... jag går till... ...
that's great, thanks a lot jättebra, tack så
mycket

Accommodation

where's the youth hostel? var ligger
vandrarhemmet?
I'd like a single/double room jag skulle vilja

ha ett enkelrum/dubbelrum
can I see it? får jag se det?
how much is it a night? hur mycket kostar
det per natt?
I'll take it jag tar det
it's too expensive, I don't want it now det
är för mycket, jag tar det inte
can I/we leave the bags here until...? kan
jag/vi få lämna väskorna här till......?
have you got har du något
...anything cheaper? ...billigare?
...with a shower? ...med dusch?

Food and drink terms

Snacks and basics

ägg egg
bröd bread
glass ice cream
keks biscuits
ost cheese
pommes chips
senap mustard
smör butter
smörgås sandwich
socker sugar
tårta cake

Meat (Kött)

biff beef
fläsk pork
hjort venison
kalvkött veal
korv sausage
köttbullar meatballs
kyckling chicken
lammkött lamb
renstek roast reindeer
skinka ham

Fish (fisk)

ansjovis anchovies
blåmusslor mussels
forell trout
hummer lobster
kaviar caviar
krabba crab
kräftor crayfish
lax salmon
makrill mackerel

räkor prawns
sill herring
sjötunga sole
strömming Baltic herring
torsk cod

Vegetables (Grönsaker)

blomkål cauliflower
bönor beans
gurka cucumber
lök onion
morötter carrots
potatis potatoes
sallad lettuce/salad
svamp mushrooms
tomater tomatoes
vitlök garlic

Fruit (Frukt)

ananas pineapple
apelsin orange
äpple apple
banan banana
citron lemon
hallon raspberry
hjortron cloudberry
jordgubbar strawberries
lingon lingonberry
päron pear
persika peach
vindruvor grapes

Culinary terms

ångkokt steamed
blodig rare
filé fillet
friterad deep fried
genomstekt well done
gravad cured
grillat/halstrat grilled
kall cold
kokt boiled
lagom medium
rökt smoked
stekt fried
ungstekt roasted/baked
varm hot

Drinks

apelsinjuice orange juice
chocklad hot chocolate
citron lemon
fruktjuice fruit juice
kaffe coffee
lättöl light beer
mellanöl medium-strong beer
mineralvatten mineral water
mjölk milk
öl beer
rödvin red wine
te tea
vatten water
vin wine

SMALL PRINT

Publishing Information
First edition 2024

Distribution
UK, Ireland and Europe
Apa Publications (UK) Ltd; sales@roughguides.com
United States and Canada
Ingram Publisher Services; ips@ingramcontent.com
Australia and New Zealand
Booktopia; retailer@booktopia.com.au
Worldwide
Apa Publications (UK) Ltd; sales@roughguides.com

Special Sales, Content Licensing and CoPublishing
Rough Guides can be purchased in bulk quantities at discounted prices. We can create special editions, personalised jackets and corporate imprints tailored to your needs. sales@roughguides.com.
roughguides.com

Printed in Czech Republic

This book was produced using **Typefi** automated publishing software.

A catalogue record for this book is available from the British Library

The publishers and authors have done their best to ensure the accuracy and currency of all the information in *Pocket Rough Guide Stockholm*, however, they can accept no responsibility for any loss, injury, or inconvenience sustained by any traveller as a result of information or advice contained in the guide.

Rough Guide Credits
Editor: Siobhan Warwicker
Cartography: Katie Bennett
Picture Editor: Tom Smyth
Layout: Pradeep Thapliyal
Original design: Richard Czapnik
Head of DTP and Pre-Press: Rebeka Davies
Head of Publishing: Sarah Clark

About the author
Annie Warren is a writer, editor, translator and occasional stand-up comedian based in the East Midlands. Her hobbies include breakfast, lunch and dinner. You can find more of her work on her website at annie-warren.com, or follow her on social media at @notanniewarren.

Acknowledgements

Annie would like to thank Visit Stockholm and Stockholm LGBT, particularly Uwern, Christina, Michelle and Anna, for a life-changing trip to Sweden and especially for teaching me the words to Helan Går. Skål! Thanks also to James Proctor, Norman Renouf, Zoe Ross, and Steve Vickers, whose work helped me immensely.

Help us update

We've gone to a lot of effort to ensure that this edition of the **Pocket Rough Guide Stockholm** is accurate and up-to-date. However, things change – places get "discovered", opening hours are notoriously fickle, restaurants and rooms raise prices or lower standards. If you feel we've got it wrong or left something out, we'd like to know, and if you can remember the address, the price, the hours, the phone number, so much the better.

   Please send your comments with the subject line "**Pocket Rough Guide Stockholm Update**" to mail@uk.roughguides.com. We'll credit all contributions and send a copy of the next edition (or any other Rough Guide if you prefer) for the very best emails.

Photo Credits

(Key: T-top; C-centre; B-bottom; L-left; R-right)

Amanda Jona/Strömma Turism & Sjöfart AB 21B
Anna Danielsson/Nationalmuseum 63
Anna Gerdén/Tekniska museet 88
Barobao 77
Blå Dörren 79
Cirkus 60
Grand Hotel 18B
Hasselbacken 61
Holger Ellgaard 90
Hotell Hasselbacken 20C, 61
Hyatt 104/105
Jean Baptiste-Beranger/ARtipelag 11B
Johan Sellgren/Historiska museet 87
Jonas André/Scenkonstmuseet 85
Katla Studios/ABBA The Museum 10
Kpa/Zuma/Shutterstock 78

Linn Ahlgren/Nationalmuseum 69
Matti Östling 66
Michela Simoncini 89
Myrorna 76
Nationalmuseum 12/13B
Ove Kaneberg/Medelhavsmuseet 40
Sara Kollberg/Skansen 20B
Shutterstock 1, 2T, 2BL, 2C, 2BR, 4, 6, 11T, 12/13T, 12B, 13C, 14B, 14T, 15B, 15T, 16B, 16T, 17B, 17T, 18T, 18C, 19T, 19C, 20T, 21T, 21C, 22/23, 25, 27, 28, 29, 30, 31, 32, 34, 39, 43, 45, 48, 50, 53, 57, 62, 65, 67, 71, 74, 80, 82, 83, 86, 93, 95, 97, 98, 99, 100, 101, 102, 103, 114/115
SuperStock 75
Thielska Galleriet 58
Tove Freij/Visit Stockholm 19B
trolvag 59
Visit Åland/Rebecka Eriksson 96

Cover: Gamla Stan **Shutterstock**

Index

NOTES

NOTES